Using Qualitative Methods in Organizational Research

Organizational Research Methods Series

edited by Larry Williams

Students, researchers, and faculty in the area of organizational studies are, in many instances, insufficiently prepared to conduct high quality research. This series addresses this problem by providing information on cutting-edge organizational research technologies and techniques. Each book offers a clear description of how the method or technique is or can be used in organizational research. Numerous organizational examples are given to facilitate the linking of the method to specific substantive questions of interest to organizational researchers. The books are appropriate for organizational researchers, faculty, and graduate students in organizational studies such as human resources management, organizational behavior, and industrial and organizational psychology.

Books in this series include:

Using Qualitative Methods in Organizational Research

Thomas W. Lee

Organizational Research Methods

SAGE Publications
International Educational and Professional Publisher
Thousand Oaks   London   New Delhi

For information:

SAGE Publications, Inc.
2455 Teller Road
Thousand Oaks, California 91320
E-mail: order@sagepub.com

SAGE Publications Ltd.
6 Bonhill Street
London EC2A 4PU
United Kingdom

SAGE Publications India Pvt. Ltd.
M-32 Market
Greater Kailash I
New Delhi 110 048 India

Printed in the United States of America

Library of Congress Cataloging-in-Publication Data

Lee, Thomas W.
    Using qualitative methods in organizational research / by Thomas W. Lee.
        p.   cm. — (Organizational research methods)
    Includes index.
    ISBN 0-7619-0806-4 (cloth: acid-free paper)
    ISBN 0-7619-0807-2 (pbk.: acid-free paper)
    1. Organizational sociology—Research. 2. Organizational behavior—Research. I. Title. II. Series: Organizational research methods (Unnumbered)
    HM131 .L386   1998
    302.3'5'072—ddc21   98-9083

This book is printed on acid-free paper.

99 00 01 02 03 04 05 7 6 5 4 3 2 1

Acquiring Editor:	Marquita Flemming
Production Editor:	Astrid Virding
Editorial Assistant:	Denise Santoyo
Designer/Typesetter:	Lynn Miyata
Indexer:	Teri Greenberg
Cover Designer:	Candice Harman

To *Janet Thompson*, my wife, lover, best friend,
and partner in life, and to *Joseph T. W. Lee*,
our best, brightest, and happiest joint venture

Contents

Series Editor's Introduction

Organizational research methodologists are conducting theoretical and empirical investigations in many areas of research design, data collection, and statistical analyses, and these efforts span both quantitative and qualitative methods. At the same time, there is evidence of increasing interest in research methods by members of the organizational scholarly community who are not methodologists. For example, special workshops and tutorials on new methodological developments have been extremely popular at professional meetings on both the regional and national level. Finally, the results of a recent review of the activities of the Research Methods Division of the Academy of Management indicate a continuing need for materials to facilitate training of organizational researchers in various areas of research methods.

This book series is intended to be a means through which substantive organizational researchers can become informed of new methodological developments. I hope that readers of books in the series will come away with fresh ideas about how to design their research, measure their variables, and conduct their data analysis. I also hope that the resulting improved methods of research will yield richer understandings of the organizational phenomena of interest.

—Larry J. Williams
University Professor of Management
Virginia Commonwealth University
Center for the Advancement of Research Methods and Analysis

Preface

When I began writing this book many months ago, I wondered what it would feel like to be finished and what I would want to say at that time. It was, after all, my first attempt at writing a book. Five minutes ago, I decided that the book was done. Many feelings and thoughts are swimming in my mind. Among these feelings is that I am greatly relieved to be done and quite pleased that I have, in fact, written a book. Much like working on a doctoral dissertation, there is that lingering doubt about whether you can really pull it all together until you're pretty far along in the process. Moreover, I feel optimism that my colleagues and their doctoral students will learn something useful and intellectually stimulating from these pages.

Among the thoughts I am having, two points merit brief mention. First, all qualitative researchers should be very explicit about their biases and personal worldviews. Thus, I want to note early on that my assumptions about this book's readership, my initial expectations, my goals for this book, and my views on the tensions between qualitative and quantitative research traditions are stated in the first half of Chapter 1. Second, the design (or flow) of this book is such that the discussion moves from more general issues in the earlier chapters to more specific topics in qualitative research in the later chapters. (Anyone who wants a quick preview of this book's structure and my intentions should see Table 1.1 and the section in Chapter 1 headed "Suggested Reading Strategies.")

Like many authors, I was surprised by how much I learned from writing a book. Frankly, I thought I knew a whole lot more about qualitative research than I actually did. Thus, there is a fair amount of personal satisfaction in learning so much more about a topic that I thought I knew pretty well; as it turns out, my scholarly arrogance was misplaced. Even more salient, however, is another surprising discovery: I had a great deal of *fun* writing this book. There were many days when I just couldn't wait to get to my computer and put more words on paper. Albeit said with hindsight, I hope that my sense of fun and some irreverence comes through to the reader.

Finally, it is imperative that I thank certain people, because without their involvement, this book would never have existed. First, I thank Dr. Larry Williams, series editor, and Ms. Marquita Flemming, senior editor at Sage Publications. They initiated this project and provided me the opportunity to write this book. Second, I thank Drs. Steven C. Currall (Rice University), Ronald Karren (University of Massachusetts, Amherst), Craig Lundberg (Cornell University), and Bill Wooldridge (University of Massachusetts, Amherst) for their insightful, thoughtful, and valuable comments. Undoubtedly, this book is vastly improved by their help. Nonetheless, any errors are completely my fault. Third, I want to thank all those people who have worked with me, as well as those who have helped me, over the years to be a better scholar. Although there are many people I should name, I will mention only two and hope that the others will understand. In particular, I thank Professor Rick Mowday (University of Oregon), who was my doctoral adviser and is now my senior colleague and good friend; and Professor Terry Mitchell (University of Washington), who is also my senior colleague and good friend. More so than any other of my fine and wonderful colleagues, they have pushed and inspired me to be a better scholar over the years. Fourth, I thank Tim Hilton and Dennis Gong for reminding me how to laugh. Finally, I thank my wife, Janet Thompson, and my son, Joseph, for providing all of the enriching intangibles in my life.

1

Introduction

In this chapter, assumptions about who will likely read this book, expectations about their reactions, and goals for this book are stated. In addition, commonly felt tensions between qualitative and quantitative researchers are summarized, and the author's opinions about these tensions are offered. Next, examples of the blending of qualitative and quantitative research are provided, and descriptions are given of how organizational researchers have actually applied qualitative methods. Finally, the book's chapters are previewed and various strategies are recommended that readers might use to approach the chapters.

Assumptions About This Book's Audience

Although its history, role, and status are well established within many social science disciplines—most notably, sociology, education, and anthropology—qualitative research remains poorly defined and not well understood among many of the targeted audience, namely, organizational scientists. Along with that label, the terms *organizational researchers* and *management researchers* will be used interchangeably throughout this volume. I seek a broad audience, and my use of these three labels should be taken to mean that the targeted audience includes *all* persons who conduct research on and in organizations (i.e., qualitatively and quantitatively oriented scholars).

It is my expectation that this book's likely readers will include many management professors and their doctoral students, who are usually housed within schools of business administration. Other potential readers may include people from more traditional liberal arts departments, such as individuals specializing in industrial and organizational psychology, organizational sociology, and organizational communication. In addition, it may also include some people from other professional schools, such as public administration, nursing, and engineering, where organizational science is often taught.

At the risk of overgeneralization, most organizational scientists are traditionally trained in, and are therefore biased toward, quantitative analysis, positivism, and theory-driven research. Indeed, I should note that I was also traditionally trained, and my research history likewise suggests those traditional biases. For example, I have actively advocated the adoption by organizational researchers of the statistical technique of survival analysis (Morita, Lee, & Mowday, 1989, 1993). Nonetheless, there seems to be a growing awareness among organizational scientists that our research problems and issues (a) mirror real-world organizational functioning, (b) are becoming increasingly complex, and (c) are getting harder to address. As suggested by the increasing number of qualitative research articles appearing in the major management journals over the past decade and by the formal research forums on qualitative methods held at national and regional meetings of the Academy of Management, many organizational researchers are becoming interested in learning about and possibly applying qualitative designs.

Two of my major goals in this book are to *inform* these management researchers about and to *advocate* the wider application of qualitative methods in organizational science. Although it may be needless to say, the management researcher's operating assumption should *not* be whether to conduct qualitative versus quantitative research. Instead, the operating issue should be, How might the best methods be applied? Thus, my hope is that this book becomes both a common shelf reference for organizational researchers and a widely assigned text in doctoral courses on research methods.

Initial Expectations

At the 1996 meetings of the Academy of Management, held in Cincinnati, Ohio, a somewhat strident confrontation occurred between the qualitative and quantitative research camps at the annual business meeting of the Research Methods Division. Moreover, this confrontation became the subject of numerous hallway conversations. About 6 months after this business meeting took place, I was asked for my opinion on what had transpired. As I saw matters, members from the qualitative camp strongly asserted that their research was neither understood nor appreciated by members of the quantitative camp, who were alleged to hold most of the established power and gatekeeper positions within the Research Methods Division. As a result, they asserted that qualitative research was underrepresented on the annual program. My interpretation of that confrontation, as well as subsequent conversations about the event with elected officials of the Research Methods Division, is that there is a great deal of heightened sensitivity among qualitative researchers about their work and contribution to organizational science. In my judgment, this heightened sensitivity remains today.

Given the existing tensions, it is my expectation that this book will receive a bimodal reaction. On the one hand, those people in the qualitative camp may be relatively unenthusiastic about this volume because they may perceive it as insufficiently deep. Much of what appears in this volume may already be known to and accepted by many sociologically and anthropologically oriented management researchers. Moreover, advocates of certain qualitative methods may feel that their particular research foci have been, albeit unintentionally, slighted (e.g., hermeneutics, the deconstructive study of texts). In addition, in this book I advocate certain rules of thumb for both qualitative and quantitative methods when applied by organizational researchers. I anticipate that some organizational researchers will object to these guidelines because qualitative and quantitative methods are often taken to be mutually exclusive at both philosophical and mechanical levels. (I discuss these differences at various places in this book.) On the other hand, it is my expectation that people in the quantitative camp may be relatively enthusiastic about this volume. Many of these organizational researchers have minimal knowledge about qualitative methods. Nonetheless, they appear to be very receptive to learning about and applying any useful tools that might facilitate their research agendas. Thus, this book may be timely for these quantitatively oriented organizational researchers.

As noted, I will not be shy about offering suggestions to organizational researchers on the application of qualitative methods. In a sense, this book may hold a "first mover advantage." That is, it can readily make recommendations concerning approaches to, judgment of, and conduct of qualitative research, in part because of the minimal knowledge about the topic among many organizational researchers. But this book holds a "first mover disadvantage" as well: There is substantial room for legitimate criticism of any suggested standards, in part because organizational scientists have less tradition in qualitative research with which to guide its application. Thus, it may be best for the reader to approach my suggested guidelines as points of discussion. There are, and should be, few canons of appropriate conduct in qualitative research.

The Goals of This Book

In this book, I present various qualitative techniques and methods of categorical data analysis. Moreover, I advocate that these techniques and methods should be blended within a program of research. Nevertheless, I do not overemphasize any individual qualitative techniques or methods of categorical data analysis, because many existing books (e.g., Yamaguchi, 1991; Yin, 1994) and monograph series (e.g., two series from Sage Publications: Qualitative Research Methods and Quantitative Applications in the Social Sciences) provide excellent treatments on specific topics.

In the aggregate, however, qualitative techniques receive substantially more coverage here than does categorical data analysis, because, in my experience, most organizational researchers have more information about and are more comfortable with quantitative than qualitative methods. Further, methods of categorical data analysis receive nonmathematical and conversational-level treatment here, because I have found that excessive formality in such discussions (including formulas, derivations, and proofs) can be quite distracting to many persons in the target audience (though some formulas are unavoidable in Chapter 6).

Thus, this book is written for the mainstream organizational scientist, whose research happens by tradition to be far more quantitative than qualitative in orientation.

Finally, I should also state at the outset that this book is not intended to be a "how-to" manual. Admittedly, Chapters 4, 5, and 6 do have something of a how-to feel to them, but more detailed how-to information can be derived from other excellent sources (e.g., Creswell, 1998; Mason, 1996; Miles & Huberman, 1994; Morgan, 1997). Instead, in this book I seek to make the traditionally quantitative researcher comfortable with qualitative methods and the traditionally qualitative researcher comfortable with categorical data analysis. It is my strong hope that in the long term, the use of both qualitative and quantitative research methods becomes common among management researchers.

Tensions Between Qualitative and Quantitative Traditions

Part of the friction between the qualitative and quantitative traditions derives from the absence of specific and agreed-upon definitions for what constitutes both qualitative and quantitative research. As a result, any attempt to summarize the very real tensions felt by many organizational researchers is akin to trying to hit a moving target. Unfortunately, the quantitative and qualitative traditions are too often oversimplified into "research with numbers versus research with no numbers." Fortunately, however, several additional distinguishing characteristics have recently been articulated by Creswell (1994), Cassell and Symon (1994), Kvale (1996), and others. (As a point of clarification for subsequent chapters, I use the terms *method* and *design* interchangeably; both refer to a study's larger plan. In addition, I use the terms *technique* and *tactic* interchangeably; these refer to the specific details and actions involved in gathering and analyzing a study's data.)

Creswell's Five Differences

Moving beyond "numbers versus no numbers," Creswell (1994, p. 5) argues that five fundamentally different assumptions separate quantitative from qualitative research. (Creswell's assertions stem from a qualitative researcher's point of view, but they do not focus on organizations; thus, these five differences should be taken as illustrative.)

First, the designs of the two kinds of research presume different realities; this is called the *ontological* assumption. Whereas quantitative researchers typically assume a single objective world, qualitative researchers typically assume that multiple subjectively derived realities can coexist. Second, the two forms of research presume different roles for the researcher (the *epistemological* assumption). Quantitative researchers commonly assume their independence from the variables under study, whereas qualitative researchers commonly assume that they must interact with their studied phenomena. Third, the two camps' values are presumed to operate differently (the *axiological* assumption). Quantitative researchers overtly act in a value-free and unbiased manner. In contrast, qualitative researchers overtly act in a value-laden and biased fashion. Fourth, the two kinds of research adopt different language styles (the *rhetorical* assumption). Quantitative researchers most often use impersonal, formal, and rule-based text, whereas qualitative researchers most often use personalized, informal, and context-based language. Fifth, the two use different research processes (the *methodological* assumption). Whereas those in the quantitative group tend to apply deduction, limited cause-effect relationships, and context-free methods, those in the qualitative group tend to apply induction, multivariate and multiprocess interactions, and context-specific methods. Thus, Creswell identifies five fundamental differences—ontology, epistemology, axioms, rhetoric, and methodology—that go far beyond the simplistic notion of numbers versus no numbers.

Cassell and Symon's Six Differences

Cassell and Symon (1994, pp. 3-7) identify six defining differences between the quantitative and qualitative methods and techniques practiced by British organizational psychologists. The first, and most superficial, difference is often taken to be "numbers versus no numbers." A more accurate way to describe this difference, however, is "quantification versus interpretation." More specifically, qualitative researchers endeavor to describe organizational phenomena. If "counting the countable" helps in that effort, then qualitative researchers should undoubtedly use numbers and quantitative analyses. Thus, this first difference can also be characterized as a "bias toward counting [held by quantitative researchers] versus counting only if clearly necessary [held by qualitative researchers]."

Second, qualitative researchers explicitly and overtly apply their own subjective interpretations to the understanding of organizational phenomena. In contrast, quantitative researchers more often seek objective (or less biased) and finely calibrated descriptions. In Cassell and Symon's (1994) view, qualitative researchers favor greater personal investment in the data, and quantitative researchers favor a more detached, impersonal orientation toward the data. It is important to note that no inference should be taken that members of either group are more (or less) involved in or committed to their research efforts.

Third, qualitative researchers often encourage substantial flexibility in research procedures. By comparison, quantitative research often appears more rule driven. Whereas quantitative researchers enter with a relatively clear mental model for their designs (e.g., laboratory experiment, field survey), qualitative researchers do not commonly enter with strong prototypical models to follow. For example, the main steps in a participant observer study are not necessarily self-evident. Qualitative researchers usually want to be maximally responsive (or reflexive) to the constraints imposed by their immediate situation and empirical data. That is, they prefer to have the maximal degree of flexibility in responding to unpredictable research problems. In contrast, quantitative researchers usually want to anticipate and eliminate problems before they occur, which can be accomplished through detailed, prespecified research designs (e.g., inclusion of experimental control groups or statistical control variables).

Fourth, qualitative researchers focus more on understanding organizational processes and less on predicting outcomes. In contrast, quantitative researchers focus more on predicting outcomes and less on process variables. Although understanding and prediction are not necessarily mutually exclusive, it is commonly held that qualitative and quantitative researchers often look at organizational events, processes, and characteristics from very different points of view.

Fifth, virtually all qualitative research is heavily grounded within the local context in which the phenomena of interest occur. As a result, generalizing empirical results to a larger population or other settings can be problematic. In contrast, quantitative research is typically presented as more context-free and therefore more generalizable. Contextual depth versus statistical generalization is most often presented as a trade-off, though neither is necessarily superior to the other.

Sixth, qualitative researchers are more explicit about participants' reactions than are quantitative researchers. Indeed, qualitative researchers recognize and integrate the effects of the research process itself (e.g., prompting, demand characteristics, intrusiveness) into the study's results much more so than do quantitative researchers.

Kvale's Differences

Although discussing qualitative research interviews, Kvale (1996) suggests that qualitative research most often focuses on the identification of meaningful categories (or parts) of organizational phenomena. As a result, qualitative research often involves content analysis and nominal (i.e., the part is absent or present) or ordinal (i.e., there is less or more of the part) calibration. In contrast, quantitative research involves more intensive calibration of organizational parts, and its analyses usually include (or presume) at least equal interval scaling.

From Kvale's perspective, the primary difference between qualitative and quantitative research appears to be which tools are applied. Kvale's position (and to some extent Creswell's, 1994, and Cassell & Symon's, 1994) suggests that the selection of appropriate tools depends upon the analytic situation. Thus, one interpretation of Kvale's position is that the two research traditions may be best suited to different types of questions. Whereas qualitative research may be better suited to questions concerning differences in categorical states, quantitative research may be better suited to questions of differences in degree within and across these categorical states. It might be noted that, with the recent advances in methods of categorical data analysis (e.g., Agresti, 1990, 1996; Bishop, Fienberg, & Holland, 1975; Cox, 1970; Fienberg, 1989), Kvale's identified differences between qualitative and quantitative research designs may be substantially smaller than commonly thought. (Methods of categorical data analysis are discussed in Chapter 6.)

Two Other Differences

Two additional tensions between the quantitative and qualitative research traditions merit brief mention. First, it is sometimes alleged that qualitative research is better suited for theory creation, whereas quantitative research is better suited for theory testing. In organizational science, this certainly appears to be true more often than not (e.g., Butterfield, Trevino, & Ball, 1996; Sutton & Hargadon, 1996), though there are exceptions (Lee, Mitchell, Wise, & Fireman, 1996). It should be noted, however, that methodologists specializing in qualitative research clearly assert that these methods can indeed accomplish both theory generation and theory testing. For example, Yin (1994) argues this point in regard to case study research, and Thomas (1993) takes the same stand regarding ethnography. Furthermore, quantitative methods can also accomplish theory creation as well. For example, a major purpose of exploratory factory analysis is to identify the underlying "latent traits" from a correlation matrix (Gorsuch, 1974). Such identification (or discovery) of underlying factors can be interpreted as a step toward quantitative theory creation. Thus, the larger literature indicates that both qualitative and quantitative research methods can be appropriately applied to create or to test organizational theories. (Qualitative methods that appear well suited for generating or testing theory are presented in Chapter 3.)

Second, many chapters and books that have been published on qualitative research methods, although typically not those that are organizationally based, may display a particular form of myopia. In particular, some sources tend to equate virtually all quantitative research with experimental design. Far more often than not, they ignore alternatives. For example, structural equation modeling (which was formerly—though loosely—labeled causal correlational analysis) and categorical data analysis are missing. It is my assertion that not only should quantitative researchers learn about and possibly apply qualitative designs (when feasible), but qualitative researchers would be well-advised to learn about and possibly apply methods of categorical data analysis (when feasible). In other words, qualitative researchers should follow Cassell and Symon's (1994) advice to "to count the countable."

Summarizing the Tensions

Two stereotypes about the differences between the qualitative and quantitative research traditions may be strongly held by organizational scientists. Qualitative research is often taken to mean inductive, theory-generating, subjective, and nonpositivist processes. In contrast, quantitative research is often taken to mean deductive, theory-testing, objective, and positivist processes. Furthermore, a few management researchers believe that these differences are so meaningfully large that one must do either qualitative or quantitative research. Simply put, it is not feasible to do both. In my judgment, however, the vast majority of organizational researchers believe that both traditions offer valuable and useful research designs and techniques that can help them to understand organizations better (e.g., McCall & Bobko, 1990). Thus, it may behoove our larger academic discipline to recognize a middle ground.

Toward a Middle Ground

Mason (1996) elegantly captures the essence of the tensions between qualitative and quantitative research with two rhetorical questions. First, she asks, How much does one believe in the reflectivity of the study's participants versus the unobtrusiveness of the data collector? Second, she asks, How much does one believe in an "ad hoc or improvisational" research design versus a scripted or more "blueprint" research orientation? In answer to both questions, qualitatively oriented researchers tend to emphasize the former and qualitative researchers tend to emphasize the latter.

Although Mason poses enlightening rhetorical questions, organizational scientists might emphasize a middle position. Most management researchers accept that organizational members actively engage, at least to some extent, in the social construction of reality and sense making (Weick, 1995). By inference, multiple subjective realities can coexist, and the desirability of qualitative research aimed at understanding these multiple realities is suggested.

Simultaneously, most management researchers also accept that a vast amount of *systematic regularity*, though not complete uniformity, occurs within organizational contexts as well (Roberts, Hulin, & Rousseau, 1978). It is this systematic regularity in employees' behaviors, interpretations, and agreement on organizational processes that allows the evolution of dominant modes, larger organizational cultures, and a "strong, agreed-upon, taken-for-granted, and virtually singular organizational reality." In other words, such systematic regularity allows people to act as if there is something akin to an objective reality. Moreover, it suggests the desirability of quantitative research aimed at understanding this subjectively determined but essentially uniform sense making.

Thus, I am advocating a middle position between (a) the assumption of an objective reality (in the physical science sense) and (b) an ongoing and constant process of interpretation, sense making, and social construction of organizational settings. Reiterating an earlier point, organizational researchers should ask whether the best method has been applied, and *not* whether qualitative or quantitative designs should be tried. Furthermore, I am also asserting the advisability of *blending* qualitative and quantitative research.

Examples of the Blending of Qualitative and Quantitative Research

Creswell (1994, pp. 177-178) proposes three general models (or designs) for blending qualitative and quantitative research. Two of these models appear quite useful for organizational research, but the third may have more limited application.

Two-Phase Design

The first model is called a *two-phase design*. Simply put, a quantitative study is followed by a qualitative study (or the reverse), and this sequencing implies comparable standards for methodological rigor (discussed in Chapter 7). For example, suppose a researcher is interested in the effects of a firm's profitability and liquidity on its research and development (R&D) intensity. Such effects are widely accepted as important by managers, public policy makers, and management researchers (e.g., Hundley, Jacobson, & Park, 1996). To understand these effects, the researcher could draw a large random sample, obtain measures of the focal variables from commercially available sources (e.g., Standard & Poor's COMPUSTAT), and then use ordinary least squares (OLS) regression (Cohen & Cohen, 1983) to examine indices of intensity in relation to indices of profitability and liquidity. Presuming statistically significant effects, the regression model would document the relative contribution of profitability and liquidity toward the prediction of R&D intensity.

Suppose further that the researcher wants a *deeper* or *richer* sense of how these and other factors affect a manager's decision on the firm's R&D intensity. She might next select a representative sample of firms from a particular industry of interest (e.g., children's computer games) and seek permission to interview the vice presidents of research and development. Because existing theory may not be sufficiently developed to guide the interview's sequence of specific questions, the researcher might adopt a more exploratory mode. In particular, she might enter these interviews with a clear agenda of topics (e.g., the roles for market research, industrial intelligence, and blind luck) that she has generated from related theory or prior interviews. Next, she might explore these topics through semistructured interviews. From these more open-ended interviews, the researcher's skill at (a) eliciting information, (b) creating provisional hypotheses, (c) tentatively testing these hypotheses in subsequent interviews, and (d) inducing preliminary thinking about formal theory would be evoked. (This example illustrates the "conversational interview," which is described in Chapter 4.)

The singular advantage of the two-phase design is that it capitalizes on the unique strengths of two traditionally separate research orientations. In particular, the quantitative study's OLS regression can inform the researcher about the calibrated effects of specific and preselected predictor variables on the dependent variable. In a complementary fashion, the qualitative study can inform the management researcher about additional variables, processes, and conditions that might surround these calibrated effects.

The singular disadvantage of the two-phase design is the potential for disjointed results. Because most organizational researchers tend to be far better trained in one or the other of the two research traditions, there is an enhanced likelihood of substantial differences in quality between the two parts of the study. For instance, quantitatively trained researchers are often insufficiently prepared to conduct qualitative interview studies, thus their efforts are likely to produce weaker qualitative data. Of course, the reverse situation may be true as well. Despite this shortcoming, however, the two-phase design may hold great promise for enhancing the body of knowledge of organizational research.

Dominant-Less Dominant Design

The second model is called the *dominant-less dominant design.* Within a qualitative study, a small quantitative component is designed into the research (or the reverse). For example, suppose an organizational researcher is interested in the tensions felt by employees when their expressed emotions differ substantially from their private emotions. As part of the research effort, the researcher might gain employment at a company widely known for its cultural control of behavior (e.g., Nordstrom, Disney). Over time, he would observe, converse with other employees, hypothesize, and record data on these emotional conflicts. Although field notes are the most immediate outcome of such data-based activities, their consistency over time (that is, their reliability—discussed in Chapter 7) is often a major concern. To make a partial check on the consistency (or reliability) of his field notes, the researcher might estimate interrater agreement. For instance, a research assistant (RA) might also gain temporary or part-time employment at the same company. The RA, who would presumably be well versed in ethnographic tactics, could observe, converse with others, hypothesize, and record an independent set of field notes on these same phenomena. Although such work is labor- and time-intensive, as are virtually all qualitative research efforts, a second RA could judge the degree of consistency across the two sets of field notes. The degree of agreement could be indexed by a kappa coefficient (Agresti, 1996), percentage of agreement, or possibly a correlation coefficient.

The major advantage of the dominant-less dominant design is its utilization of the unique strengths of one research tradition while capitalizing on selected attributes of the other. This design tends to minimize the risk of the researcher's misapplying sometimes very different methods, tactics, and philosophical traditions.

The major disadvantage of the dominant-less dominant design is that quantitative researchers are often uncomfortable with qualitative techniques. As a result, they may be prone to misapply certain qualitative tactics. (Of course, the reverse situation could exist as well.) Moreover, some qualitative management researchers, though certainly not all, believe that it is fundamentally wrong, at a basic philosophical level, to mix modes. Nevertheless, the dominant-less dominant design may lend itself quite effectively to many research situations. As such, it may be the most practical of the three designs.

Mixed-Methodology Design

The third model is the *mixed-methodology design*. Within a single study, multiple qualitative and quantitative techniques might be applied. By selecting multiple techniques, the researcher creates a set of complementary data-gathering activities that compensate for the weaknesses of individual tactics. The data thus collected are thought to be descriptively rich (and therefore quite informative) and quantitatively meaningful.

Certainly, mixed-methodology designs have great potential, but their conceptual and mechanical complexity can be overwhelming. In addition, there remain many qualitatively oriented researchers who believe that such mixing may not be fundamentally possible. Because this model seems ill-suited for organizational research, I will not give an example here. (Marshall & Rossman, 1995, pp. 99-104, provide an empirical example of an approximate mixed-methodology design.) Throughout this book, I will offer more examples of the two-phase and dominant-less dominant designs than of the mixed-methodology design.

Qualitative Research in Management Journals, 1984-1994

Given my goals of encouraging the wider application of qualitative methods in organizational science as well as the blending of qualitative and quantitative designs, it may be informative if I can impart a sense of how qualitative research has actually been applied in management research. Such knowledge may serve as a useful point of departure. That is, it may provide an awareness of where organizational research is with respect to the application of qualitative methods, and where it may need to go.

Larsson and Lowendahl (1996) were interested in whether the breadth and richness of qualitative methods and tactics are reflected in its actual use among organizational researchers. They conducted a meta-analytic review of the espoused and actual applications of qualitative methods in management research. Larsson and Lowendahl defined the "top-ranked management journals" as the *Academy of Management Journal, Administrative Science Quarterly, Organizational Science,* and *Strategic Management Journal.* They conducted a literature search among the articles published from 1984 to 1994, and judged the following 12 studies to be qualitative: Bartunek (1984), Biggart and Hamilton (1984), Adler and Adler (1988), Gersick (1988), Eisenhardt (1989), Barley (1990), Dutton and Dukerich (1991), Hamel (1991), Elsbach and Sutton (1992), Barker (1993), Burgelman (1994), and Greenwood, Hinings, and Brown (1994).

A detailed inspection of these studies revealed a very narrow range of qualitative designs. In particular, three citations were most often offered as given studies' methodological justification. Glaser and Strauss's (1967) now classic book on grounded theory was the most common methodological citation. Eisenhardt's (1989) case study research design on the speed in strategic decision making was the reference cited next most often (Larsson & Lowendahl, 1996, suggest that Eisenhardt's study appears to be moving toward the status of a "classic work"). Finally, Yin's (1984) book on case study research was the methodological reference cited third most often.

Although the norms in management research heavily emphasize the testing of preexisting theory, 11 of these 12 studies sought to generate theory; only Greenwood et al. (1994) tested theory. In addition, 6 of the studies conducted single-case research, 2 studies involved two cases, and 4 studies involved more than three cases. Virtually all of these studies were longitudinal and averaged 12 months for data collection, with a range of 1 to 23 months.

Disturbing Observations

Larsson and Lowendahl (1996) report two somewhat disturbing observations. First, although widely cited, the three common methodological citations—with particular reference to Glaser and Strauss—were more often made for purposes of scholarly legitimation than for substantive guidance on what should actually be done (e.g., "getting it past the reviewers"). To the extent this observation reflects reality, organizational researchers may not be utilizing methods of qualitative research to their fullest advantage.

Second, Larsson and Lowendahl (1996) observed that the studies' actual methods of data collection were not always made clear. Given the strong norms about reporting the fine details of research methods in management journals, such poor description is quite surprising, particularly when one considers that "rich description" is a major reason for doing qualitative research in the first place. Nonetheless, most studies gathered information through personal interviews; there were as few as 16 and as many as 219, and most interviews lasted about 2 hours in duration. Only Barley (1990) and Eisenhardt (1989) report supplementing their qualitative data with questionnaires.

Overall, Larsson and Lowendahl (1996) note, they were quite surprised by the difference between the espoused and the actual applications of qualitative research by organizational researchers. First, a particular method—most often the case study—appeared justified by citation per se rather than by the apparent connection between a given citation and what appeared to be actually done. Second, prior publication of a given method application was often taken as an acceptable proxy for valid research method. Third, descriptions of the studies' data analysis seemed quite weak. That is, general outlines were commonly provided that included terse description of Glaser and Strauss's (1967), Eisenhardt's (1989), or Yin's (1984) methods. However, it remained a "magical leap from data collection to generated theory found among the methodologies-in-use" (Larsson & Lowendahl, 1996, p. 11).

In sum, Larsson and Lowendahl (1996) conclude that both the actual and the reported qualitative research designs employed by organizational scientists remain largely uncodified. Furthermore, they suggest that until some agreement emerges on standards for qualitative research in the organizational sciences, major advances in knowledge and the application of qualitative methods will not likely occur. Thus, a major purpose of this book is to provide direction toward this codification for the management sciences.

Comment

Larsson and Lowendahl's (1996) effort at describing the applications of qualitative methods in organizational research can be said to be somewhat narrow, because, for example, their definition of "top-ranked management journals" can be debated (perhaps endlessly). Larsson and Lowendahl do, however, offer a broad-based, snapshot view, albeit a disturbing one, of how many organizational scientists approach, define, and apply qualitative methods.

In a nutshell, organizational researchers appear to take a very narrow view of qualitative research. They tend to apply qualitative methods in order to generate propositions, and tend not to use these methods (as much) to test these propositions. They also tend to rely on interviews and participant observation methods in particular, and tend not to use (as much) more objective techniques (e.g., analysis of documents and artifacts). As such, it may be timely for organizational scientists to take a deeper look at methods and tactics of qualitative research for both generating and testing management theories.

Overview of This Volume

The intended flow across this book's chapters is a move from the more general to the more specific. Chapter 2 provides broad and overall descriptions of qualitative research. Chapter 3 moves to the decision concerning whether or not to use qualitative methods and also presents an overview of four specific research designs. Chapters 4 and 5 give quite detailed information on how to collect and analyze qualitative data. Chapter 6 presents statistical methods for when it becomes feasible and desirable to apply quantitative analysis to qualitative data. Chapter 7 articulates the critical roles of reliability and validity. Finally, Chapter 8 offers conclusions and some recommendations for those who write journal articles that report qualitative studies. Summary information about Chapters 2 through 8 is provided in Table 1.1.

Additional Details

Chapter 2 presents the general domain and components of qualitative research. Furthermore, the main thrust of this chapter is to answer the

TABLE 1.1 Summary of Subsequent Chapters

Chapter	Primary Questions
2. Generic Qualitative Research Design	What are the major domains and components of qualitative research?
3. When to Use Qualitative Research and Exemplary Methods for Generating and Testing Theory	How does one begin qualitative research? What specific designs might be adopted?
4. Specific Techniques for Focus Groups, Case Study Research, and Conversational Interviews	What does one actually do when conducting qualitative research?
5. Generic Techniques for Qualitative Research	
6. Count the Countable	Which methods of categorical data analysis are likely to be useful in the quantitative analysis of qualitative data?
7. The Cardinal Concepts of Reliability and Validity	How does one judge the quality of qualitative research?
8. Conclusions	What should be reported in a qualitative research manuscript that is targeted for a management journal?

question, What are the major domains and components of qualitative research? Organizational examples are provided throughout the chapter.

Chapter 3 presents the macro methodological or design issues that arise in the conduct of qualitative research. In addition, the chapter includes discussion of specific research designs that are judged well suited for generating theory and other designs that are judged well suited for testing theory. There are two main issues discussed in Chapter 3: (a) How does one begin qualitative research? and (b) What specific designs might one adopt?

Chapters 4 and 5 detail specific techniques for data collection and analysis commonly used in qualitative research. More so than the others, these chapters adopt a how-to orientation. The main goal for Chapters 4 and 5 is to answer the question, What does one actually do when conducting qualitative research?

Chapter 6 provides an overview of specific methods of categorical data analysis. In particular, four indices for association, five forms of correlation, and log linear and logistic models are described. My intent is to present a collection of quantitative tools that may be somewhat unfamiliar to organizational researchers but that lend themselves to qualitative study. The primary aim of Chapter 6 is to answer the question, Which methods of categorical data analysis are likely to be useful in the quantitative analysis of qualitative data?

Chapter 7 presents a discussion of the conventional standards for reliability and validity, and applies these traditional concepts to qualitative designs. The main issue addressed in this chapter is, How does one judge the quality of qualitative research? Throughout this volume, I assert that reliability and validity are concepts that can and should be applied to qualitative research. Furthermore, these concepts are—and should be—the main standards used to evaluate qualitative designs and analyses.

In Chapter 8, I offer some conclusions and a summary of the preceding chapters. In addition, this chapter is intended for readers and journal reviewers of manuscripts reporting qualitative organizational research. It presents 42 questions that a reader should readily be able to answer after an initial reading of such a journal submission. Chapter 8's main purpose is to answer the question, What should be reported in a qualitative research manuscript that is targeted for a management journal?

Suggested Reading Strategies

At this point, you have presumably read most of Chapter 1. Ideally, you should read this book carefully from beginning to end. Alternatively, there are several other effective reading strategies. Organizational researchers who are familiar with qualitative methods but less so with categorical data analysis might quickly read Chapters 2 through 5, to get a sense of how I approach qualitative research, and then read Chapters 6 through 8 more carefully. Organizational researchers who are familiar with categorical data analysis but less so with qualitative research might quickly read Chapters 6 and 7, to get a sense of how I approach quantitative methods, and then read Chapters 2 through 5 and Chapter 8 more carefully. Because of the somewhat controversial nature of Chapter 7 (as far as research methods can be controversial, that is), I recommend that everyone read that chapter carefully at some point.

All in all, my strong recommendation is that you read at a comfortable pace. You can go back and reread particular chapters for any details you may have missed. Better still, you may want to read some of the works cited repeatedly throughout this volume (e.g., Miles & Huberman, 1994) to gain more comprehensive exposure to qualitative research. Whatever course you take, just read. As you do, think about how the topics in this book might apply to your own work in particular and to organizational science in general.

2

Generic Qualitative
Research Design

*This chapter provides an overview of the major domains (or categories)
of qualitative research as practiced in several social sciences and identifies
four underlying themes. The main components (or parts) of qualitative
research designs are also described, and two underlying decisions are
identified. Key decisions that must be made regarding the application of
qualitative research are then presented. Examples from the organizational sciences and the author's opinions are offered throughout the
chapter.*

Overview of the Major Domains
of Qualitative Research Design

Like identifying the tensions between the qualitative and quantitative
traditions, attempting to describe the major categories of qualitative
research is akin to trying to hit a moving target. In particular, it is often
difficult to classify studies into definitionally and conceptually coherent
categories, because most qualitative studies routinely apply multiple
techniques. For example, both interviews and observations are often
conducted within a single study (e.g., Brown & Eisenhardt, 1997), a
qualitative researcher's participation can vary from direct involvement
to hands-off observation (e.g., Adler & Adler, 1988), and a combination
of qualitative interviews and quantitatively analyzed questionnaires

TABLE 2.1 The Major Domains of Qualitative Research Design

Miles and Huberman's (1994) domains
 1. Participant observer
 2. Nonparticipant observer
 3. Interviewing
 4. Archival

Marshall and Rossman's (1995) domains
 1. Neutral domains
     a. Human ethnology
     b. Ecological psychology
     c. Holistic ethnography
     d. Cognitive anthropology
     e. Ethnography of communication
     f. Symbolic interaction

 2. Political domains
     a. Democratic evaluation
     b. Neo-Marxist ethnography
     c. Feminist research
     d. Participatory research

Creswell's (1994) domains
 1. Ethnography
 2. Grounded theory
 3. Case studies
 4. Phenomenological studies

Four Underlying Themes
 1. Qualitative research occurs in natural settings.
 2. Qualitative data derive from the participants' perspective.
 3. Qualitative research designs are flexible (i.e., reflexive).
 4. Instrumentation, observation methods, and modes of analysis are not standard.

may be applied within a single study (i.e., a two-phase design; e.g., Human & Provan, 1997).

Over the past three decades, several attempts have been made to categorize the major domains of qualitative research. Although few have had fully satisfying results, these successive efforts have produced some accumulating level of agreement on the scope of qualitative methods. Below, I discuss three recent and cumulative efforts to categorize the major domains of qualitative research: those of Miles and Huberman (1994), Marshall and Rossman (1995), and Creswell (1994). Table 2.1 summarizes these major domains.

It should be noted that the taxonomies presented below were not derived from management research. Nevertheless, they have great heuristic value. In the second part of this chapter, I describe the major components (or parts) of qualitative research design. (In line with my strategy of moving from the more general to the more specific in this volume, how-to details concerning specific qualitative methods and techniques are described in Chapters 4 and 5.)

Miles and Huberman's Domains

In their highly influential book *Qualitative Data Analysis,* Miles and Huberman (1994, pp. 6-7) describe qualitative research as falling into four major domains or categories (they use the term *strategies*): participant observer, nonparticipant observer, interviewing, and archival research. Each domain uses different and thereby distinguishing methods. In addition, each domain contains several subdomains (or substrategies, in Miles & Huberman's terms). Within each subdomain, particular designs are identified. Thus, a particular strategy can contain certain substrategies, which, in turn, can contain specific designs.

Participant observation. The first, and perhaps the most widely known, domain (or strategy) is participant observation, which comprises two subdomains (or substrategies). The first subdomain is ethnography; this includes the specific designs of community studies, ethnology, anthropological life histories, and microethnographies. The second subdomain is the field study, which includes the specific designs of phenomenology, poststructuralism, and enthnomethodology. For example, Van Maanen (1975) followed a participant observation strategy in studying the dynamics of police life. In particular, he trained formally and worked unofficially as a city police officer. In a similar vein, Sutton (1991) followed a participant observation strategy in studying the expressed emotions of bill collectors. More specifically, he worked as an actual bill collector, and through that experience he was able to converse with, interview, and observe bill collectors to gather data on their expressed emotions and other behaviors. In both these studies, data were collected in the naturally occurring contexts of the phenomena of interest.

Nonparticipant observation. The second domain is nonparticipant observation, and its specific designs include observer studies, human ethnology, and nonreactive research. For instance, Adler and Adler (1988) studied the development of intense loyalties held by college basketball players over a 5-year period. Whereas one of the researchers assumed a passive observational role, the other assumed an informal but active membership as the "team's sociologist," as well as the unofficial status of assistant coach. Because neither researcher was an actual basketball player who experienced the intense loyalty studied, this magnificent study's design can be deemed more nonparticipant than participant (though I may be splitting hairs at this point).

Interviewing. The third domain is interviewing, and it may be the most common qualitative method practiced in organizational research. Its specific designs include investigative journalism, biographies, and oral histories. For instance, Butterfield, Trevino, and Ball (1996) studied managers' perceptions of the use of punishment. Through the critical incidents interview method (Gatewood & Feild, 1994, pp. 361-364), they generated examples of particularly effective and ineffective experiences with punishment. Based on these personal stories, they developed a conceptual model they call the "inductive model of punishment from the manager's perspective."

Archival. The final domain is archival, and its specific designs include histories, content analysis, and literary criticism. For example, Ross and Staw (1986) studied the escalation of commitment to a failing course of action by reading hundreds of newspaper articles, press releases, and official documents, along with interviews of key participants, on British Columbia's decision to host Expo '86 in Vancouver. As a result, they generated a fascinating narrative that may well explain how the process of escalating commitment occurred over time on a multimillion-dollar project that was under the scrutiny of worldwide media coverage.

Marshall and Rossman's Domains

Marshall and Rossman (1995, pp. 2-3) suggest that qualitative research can be divided into 10 major domains, which are distinguished by their different philosophical orientations. In 4 of these domains, the researcher is seen as taking an explicitly activist (or an advocate's) role; in the other 6 domains, the researcher is seen as taking a more neutral role.

The neutral domains. In the first of the neutral domains, *human ethnologists* seek to understand naturally occurring behavior. In the second, *ecological psychologists* focus on the effects of interactions between individuals and their environments on the individuals' behavior. In both approaches, behavioral observations are typically gathered and then are analyzed quantitatively. Third, *holistic ethnographers* attempt to uncover and document the perspectives of the subjects of interest, usually through participant observation methods. Fourth, *cognitive anthropologists* assume that individuals organize their perspectives into coherent schemata, and that researchers can learn about these mental maps through in-depth interviews, with quantitative analyses typically following. Fifth, researchers who practice the *ethnography of communication* concentrate on understanding the verbal and nonverbal patterns among their target subjects. In this domain, participant observation and audio or video recording of individuals' interactions are commonly applied. Sixth, *symbolic interactionists* direct attention to individuals' sense making.

The political domains. In stark contrast to Marshall and Rossman's neutral domains are their overtly political domains, which stem primarily from educational research. First, *democratic evaluators* reject the quantitative methods and notions of authoritarian researchers. Instead, they aim to become facilitators of whatever underlying process is currently under study. Second, *neo-Marxist ethnographers* focus on radical modes of schooling and the political and social forces that resist or encourage their adoption in schools. Thus, these researchers intentionally take the advocate's role. Third, *feminist researchers* draw on feminist thought and action research. In particular, they focus on gender bias found in educational institutions, processes, and values. They begin with the assumption that gender bias is already operating, and then seek to understand the nature and effects of this prevalent and ongoing bias. Fourth, *participatory researchers* focus on change efforts; this domain is akin to the notion of organizational development.

Comment. In many of Marshall and Rossman's six neutral domains, both qualitative and quantitative techniques are often applied (or blended) within given studies. Thus, the distinctions between domains can often become blurred. Most important, however, is that this blurring has led some qualitative researchers to recommend de-emphasizing any demarcation between qualitative and quantitative research. Instead, both methods have their legitimate roles in organizational science. To reiterate an earlier point (and at the risk of beating a dead horse), it can only benefit organizational science if researchers apply both qualitative and quantitative designs in exploring research issues.

Furthermore, feminist traditions have been applied in management studies over many decades (Fondas, 1997). In contrast, the three other activist traditions have not had major effects on organizational research. Excepting the feminists' influence, I do not anticipate any significant effects from these political domains on mainstream organizational science. Whereas the qualitative tradition of relatively neutral, nonpolitical research methods fits closely with current mainstream organizational science, the overtly political domains do not. (It has also been my experience that the nonpolitical domains tend to be much more tolerant of quantitative methods than are the more political domains.)

Creswell's Domains

Creswell (1994, pp. 11-12) divides the domains of qualitative research into four major categories. Like Miles and Huberman (1994), he follows a methods-oriented theme. First, *ethnographers* study intact cultural groups in their natural settings over long periods of time (e.g., Van Maanen, 1975). Data are typically observationally based, subjectively interpreted, and contextually specific. In addition, ethnographic designs are described as quite flexible (or reflexive), because researchers often need to respond differently to varying situationally imposed constraints (e.g., funding agencies' rules). Second, researchers using *grounded theory* derive theory (or conceptual propositions) from the data themselves, through a multistep process (e.g., Sutton & Hargadon, 1996). These researchers engage in a continual process of inferring categories, testing their inferences against subsequent data, revising the inferred categories, and retesting the revised inferences against subsequent data. The ultimate outcome of this sequential process is well-conceived theory (or conceptual propositions) that is heavily grounded in data. Third, researchers who use *case studies* focus on one or a few entities in substantial depth (e.g., Yan & Gray, 1994). That is, these researchers study intensely, for an extended period of time, particular cases' main events, processes, and outcomes, which occur within very specific contextual boundaries.

Fourth, researchers involved in *phenomenological studies* attempt to understand the "lived experiences" of their participants (e.g., Adler & Adler, 1988). These researchers follow small numbers of persons (or other entities) extensively and intensively for sustained periods of time. Through such in-depth study, Creswell suggests, researchers can come to understand more fully their subjects' patterns, relationships, interpretations, attitudes, and behaviors.

Four Underlying Themes
From These Sets of Domains

I should note again that the domains described in this chapter are not specific to organizational research; rather, they are generic to several fields in the social sciences. Nonetheless, four distinctive themes appear evident. First, qualitative research occurs in natural settings. For management research, then, organizational or field settings are likely necessary for qualitative research. Traditional laboratory designs, simulations, and profile (e.g., "paper people") studies appear less suitable (though they are not completely inappropriate) for qualitative designs in organizational science.

Second, the empirical data from a qualitative study involve and derive from the participants' experiences within that natural setting. More specifically, these experience-based data can derive from (a) the researchers' interpretations, (b) the participants themselves, or (c) passive or active participation methods. Regardless of the source, the phenomena of interest center on the interpretations, sense making, and "lived" experiences of the involved persons. For management research, these experiences would most likely derive from organizational participants, such as managers, permanent employees, contingent employees, contractors, suppliers, and customers.

Third, qualitative research designs are flexible. In comparison with traditional experimentation or longitudinal survey designs, qualitative designs allow a researcher to adjust the ongoing data collection methods and modes of analysis much more quickly to respond to context specific constraints. Because most organizational scientists have experienced context-based (or site) problems, it may be this characteristic of flexibility (often called reflexivity) that most disturbs quantitatively oriented management researchers *and* draws them to qualitative research.

Fourth, in qualitative research, instrumentation, methods of observation, and modes of analysis are not standardized. These elements vary widely across studies. For the traditionally trained management researcher who holds a strong preference for reliable and well-validated measures (e.g., Schwab, 1980), the absence of standard instruments may cause substantial discomfort.

Major Components of Qualitative Research Design

In comparison with the modest agreement on the major domains of qualitative research (and their underlying themes), there is substantial disagreement regarding its major components. Nonetheless, my task in this section is to convey a sense of the parts that constitute a generic qualitative research design. Below, I discuss three recent efforts to categorize the major components of qualitative research undertaken by Marshall and Rossman (1995), Maxwell (1996), and Coffey and Atkinson (1996). Table 2.2 summarizes these major components. Once again, I should note that the following descriptions derive from several areas of the social sciences; none is specific to management research.

Marshall and Rossman's Components

Marshall and Rossman (1995, pp. 111-119) limit their description of the major components of qualitative research to a grounded theory approach. They imply that theory (or conceptual propositions) should be generated from empirical data, and they depict five interrelated parts. Each conveys the dynamic theme of reducing the amount of raw data while simultaneously increasing coherent interpretation.

First, the qualitative researcher must *organize* the raw data. In particular, the data must be structured such that they can be manipulated readily during analysis. Often, for example, the raw data consist of behavioral observations, verbal comments, and the subjective interpretations of these behaviors and comments (manifested as field notes). Depending upon the quantity of data, the observations, comments, and interpretations might be transcribed onto 3-by-5 cards and physically arrayed on

TABLE 2.2 The Major Components of Qualitative Research Design

---

Marshall and Rossman's (1995) components
  1. The qualitative researcher must *organize* all of the data.
  2. The qualitative researcher must *generate* themes, categories, and patterns from the data.
  3. The qualitative researcher must empirically *test* the generated themes, categories, and patterns with additional data.
  4. The qualitative researcher must *discount* potential alternative explanations.
  5. The qualitative researcher must *prepare* a research report.

Maxwell's (1996) components
  1. The purpose
  2. The conceptual context
  3. The research question
  4. Methods and tactics
  5. Validity
  6. The rubber band metaphor

Coffey and Atkinson's (1996) components
  1. Taxonomic approaches to describing components are potentially misleading.
  2. The qualitative researcher must practice *disciplined flexibility.*

Two underlying themes
  1. Qualitative research is a process of data reduction that simultaneously enhances the data's meaning.
  2. There is little standardization of instruments or procedures.

---

a tabletop to reflect some preliminary conceptual structure (e.g., a Q-sort). This imposed (or emergent) organization lends itself to straightforward data manipulation through the physical movement of the cards on the tabletop. Some word processing packages and other software designed for qualitative data analysis make possible the computer equivalent of physically recording, arraying, and moving the data.

Second, the qualitative researcher must *generate* themes, categories, and patterns based on the raw data, which can be reflected in the movement of the above-mentioned 3-by-5 cards. Of the five parts, this component may be the most demanding. It requires creativity, tolerance for ambiguity, and inductive reasoning. In essence, the researcher must impose meaning onto the data and thereby engage a preliminary (or emergent) theory. Mechanically, the researcher arranges, ponders, rearranges, ponders again, and arranges once more the 3-by-5 cards. At some point, the researcher should evolve a taxonomy that (a) is internally consistent, (b) fits with existing knowledge about the phenomenon of interest, and (c) is empirically testable.

Third, the qualitative researcher must empirically *test* any and all emergent hypotheses about themes, categories, and patterns (e.g., the structure depicted by the 3-by-5 cards). Mechanically, the researcher tests these hypotheses against data collected (potentially) concurrently with or (ideally) subsequent to his or her hypothesizing. Although quantitative analysis typically is not employed, it cannot be overemphasized that the logic of grounded theory demands intensive data-based testing and that quantitative analysis may be conducted at many points during a qualitative study. For example, the qualitative researcher might judge whether the subsequently gathered data fit with the predetermined taxonomy. Depending upon the nature of the data, such judgments can vary from the completely subjective to a chi-square test of goodness of fit (discussed in Chapter 6).

Fourth, the qualitative researcher must *discount* potential alternative explanations. Much like any traditional social scientist, the qualitative researcher is obligated to construct the most logically consistent and parsimonious empirical case possible for the emergent set of hypotheses (or theory). Mechanically, the researcher must also test the specific taxonomy he or she has asserted, as represented by a particular combination of 3-by-5 cards, against many alternative taxonomies, as represented by other combinations of the 3-by-5 cards. Through an iterative process, support should emerge for a dominant structure (i.e., theory).

Fifth, the researcher must write a report on the study and submit it for publication; the report will then undergo peer review and probably revision before it is ultimately published. Because the focus of this book is on research design and not publication, I will not discuss the crafting of a research report here, although I want to acknowledge the importance of this work to the research process. It cannot be overemphasized that the burden falls upon the qualitative researcher to describe fully the four steps described above and to convince the reader in a compelling fashion that these steps were accomplished. If a researcher cannot produce a descriptively rich and compelling report on his or her qualitative work, the study should not merit journal pages. (A brief discussion of research reports is presented in Chapter 8.)

Maxwell's Components

In contrast to Marshall and Rossman's (1995) grounded theory logic, Maxwell (1996, pp. 4-6) offers a five-part general model for the components of qualitative research. His first part concerns the *purpose* of the research. Specifically, Maxwell asks, why is the study important to some person or group, and what are its tangible outcomes (e.g., basic versus applied research)? The second component involves *conceptual contexts.* That is, what information guides or informs the study? Is it the researcher's experience, existing theory and research, pilot studies, or thought experiments? The third part is the *research question* itself: What specifically is being answered by the study, and how do the study's questions interrelate? The fourth part consists of the *methods and tactics* applied. What are the data to be collected, and what are the methods of data collection and analysis? Finally, *validity* must be addressed—in particular, how might the research be wrong, and how might these potential alternatives be discounted? (The issues of reliability and validity are addressed in Chapter 7.)

Furthermore, Maxwell (1996) sees the connections among the five parts he describes as flexible, like rubber bands. Although the parts themselves may not be unique to either qualitative or quantitative research, Maxwell argues, the rubber band metaphor is novel. The metaphor makes it explicit that, in comparison with experimentally based research, qualitative research does not hold to rule-driven designs. On the one hand, the components make up an integrated whole; on the other hand, although some changes to one or more parts can affect other components, some changes need not necessarily affect other parts. If too much pressure (or change) is applied to a study, however, the rubber bands connecting the components can snap.

Coffey and Atkinson's Components

In substantial disagreement with Marshall and Rossman (1995) and Maxwell (1996), Coffey and Atkinson (1996) argue that (a) qualitative research occurs in numerous forms, (b) qualitative researchers themselves cannot agree on what to call these forms, and (c) taxonomic approaches can become too easily misleading. Coffey and Atkinson assert that it is difficult to describe the major components of qualitative research because a variety of analytic strategies can be legitimately used within a single research project. That said, however, these authors hasten to caution that qualitative research should not be taken to mean the absence of logic or guidelines (i.e., a mentality of "anything goes").

Although data analysis in qualitative research can be cyclical, creative, or even artful, Coffey and Atkinson argue that such research requires "disciplined flexibility."

Two Underlying Themes
From These Sets of Components

As may be evident, there is substantial disagreement concerning the major components of qualitative research. Two points appear to stand out, however. First, regardless of its specific nature and the labels used for particular components, qualitative research should be seen as a process of data reduction that simultaneously enhances the data's meaning (Marshall & Rossman, 1995). Because of this emphasis on data reduction, many qualitative researchers may tend to focus too much on issues of theory generation. It is important to note that qualitative research lends itself to both theory generation and theory testing.

Second, qualitative research includes little in the way of standardized instruments and procedures (Miles & Huberman, 1994). Instead, it is most often the case that researchers themselves constitute their studies' primary "measuring instruments." For example, researchers' judgments often constitute their studies' raw data (e.g., manifested as field notes). Nonetheless, Coffey and Atkinson's (1996) warning should resonate: Qualitative research should not be seen as a case of "anything goes." The issues of reliability and validity should be applied in the evaluation of qualitative research.

Key Decisions

Although there has been substantial disagreement on how best to describe the components of qualitative research design, Mason (1996) offers an insightful way to approach this subject. The components of a qualitative study may be classified according to whether the researcher might best take the obtained data *literally, interpretatively,* or *reflexively.* In other words, the qualitative researcher should begin a study's design with a clear notion of how to make sense of the data.

Literal Interpretation of Data

When a study's data are taken literally, the meanings of observations, verbal comments, participants' sense making, and contextual pressures on the participants' experiences are taken at face value. In this case the researcher broadly accepts the participants' honesty, sincerity, and insights. Perhaps because the researcher employs little induction, theory creation and theory testing become relatively straightforward and move conceptually toward deduction. For example, organizational researchers often apply the critical incidents technique (Gatewood & Feild, 1994, pp. 361-364) to learn about employees' perceptions of their job performance. In interviews, employees describe particularly good and bad examples of their work performance. If taken literally, these examples would be interpreted as reasonably close approximations of the employees' actual good and bad work behaviors.

Interpreted Data

When a study's data are taken interpretatively, the researcher must induce their meaning. Although face-value interpretations of data can still be appropriate, the qualitative researcher likely enters into this analysis with the intent of "reading between the lines." That is, the researcher infers what the participant "really means," based not only on overt observations, verbal comments, the participant's sense making, and contextual pressures, but also on what the researcher interprets (or judges) these entities to mean. The participant's honesty, sincerity, and insights may be taken at face value, but "meaning" must be imposed by the researcher. Returning to the critical incidents example, the researcher might interpret the employee's descriptions in relation to what the researcher already knows about job performance in general or the performance of the particular employee being interviewed (e.g., there may be reason to suspect the interviewee's motives). With interpreted data, the researcher (a) makes judgments about the goodness, believability, or veracity of the examples and (b) embeds these descriptions into his or her emerging ideas about the nature of the individual's job performance.

Comment. A word of caution may be in order. Although I have never actually worked as an operator in a nuclear power plant, I have experienced (or rather endured) many (seemingly countless) hours listening to these operators' stories, watching operators doing their jobs, and talking to numerous other people who work alongside these operators. As a result, I sometimes fell into the (false) feeling that I knew the job of nuclear power plant operator better than the people who actually did it for a living. When a researcher reaches such a point, he or she may be too deeply enmeshed within the study; this can result in the potentially serious problem of overinterpretation of the data.

Reflexive Data

When a study's data are taken reflexively, the researcher must employ even more induction and interpersonal sensitivity to determine their meaning. In addition to reading between the lines, the researcher must enter with the intent of determining the meanings of observations, verbal comments, participants' sense making, and contextual pressures on the participants' experiences from particular perspectives. These perspectives can include one or more of the following: the researcher's role (e.g., basic or applied research), the researcher's position (e.g., university professor, management consultant, internal staff member), and the interaction of role and position (e.g., neutral, advocate, friendship based, trusted, outsider stranger). Moreover, the researcher is viewed as free to impose, a priori, a political agenda (e.g., neo-Marxism), pragmatic concerns (e.g., action research or organizational development), as well as philosophical viewpoints (e.g., feminist theory). Depending upon these researcher decisions, specific design and analysis issues follow.

For example, Loscocco (1997) studied differences in work-family linkages among self-employed women and men. She conducted 30 in-depth interviews that were more open-ended than structured in nature. From these interviews, she induced the following underlying themes to explain what her interviewees said (or what she took them to mean to say): work-family boundaries, parenthood and work-family linkages, gender and the provider role, and life stages. Whereas these themes appeared to derive from what the interviewees said, the explanations for why and how these themes were important in the lives of working people were ultimately *imposed* from the researcher's knowledge of existing theory, empirical research, and intuitive speculations. It is important to note that reflexive interpretation of data requires that researchers have substantial confidence in both their understanding of the phenomena of interest and their own creative talents.

Comment

The interpretative orientation fits best with the prevailing values practiced in organizational research. Typically, most management researchers are quite aware and sensitive to issues involving respondent bias. As such, they would be unlikely to accept broad and literal interpretations from their respondents. Moreover, most organizational researchers are unlikely trained or insufficiently experienced as clinicians to treat their data reflexively. As a result, they would be uncomfortable imposing reflexive (e.g., political) interpretations. Thus, interpretative modes of qualitative research seem most likely to be used in by organizational scientists.

In closing, it is worth reiterating that most attempts to describe the major domains and components of qualitative research have been somewhat unsatisfying. In defining these groupings, much of the richness that makes qualitative research so attractive is often lost. I agree with Coffey and Atkinson's (1996) sentiments that the diversity, depth, and insight that are so often gleaned from qualitative research cannot be easily conveyed. Nevertheless, the emerging underlying themes discussed above (and summarized in Tables 2.1 and 2.2), coupled with the above "key decisions," may represent movement toward a more satisfying and richer description of qualitative research within organizational science.

When to Use Qualitative Research and Exemplary Methods for Generating and Testing Theory

3

This chapter first addresses when to use qualitative research designs. Then, two methods that are particularly well suited for the creation of theory, grounded theory and focus groups, are described. This is followed by description of two other methods that are particularly well suited for testing theory: case study research and conversational interviews. Throughout the chapter, examples and the author's opinions are offered.

When to Use Qualitative Research

From the discussion in Chapter 2, we can infer that three major characteristics of qualitative research are extensive and intensive: (a) time spent by researchers physically in their field sites; (b) researchers' contact with their sites' participants, operations, and activities; and (c) researchers' efforts directed toward understanding these participants, operations, and activities. Moreover, qualitative research is often characterized as producing an overwhelming amount of data, which the researcher must expend considerable effort to reduce (Yin, 1994). Thus, Miles and Huberman (1994) suggest that qualitative research seems most appropriate

TABLE 3.1 When to Use Qualitative Research

Miles and Huberman's (1994) considerations
  1. Local grounding
  2. Richness and holism
  3. Sustained period and causality
  4. Lived meanings

Marshall and Rossman's (1995) recommendations
  1. Exploratory purposes: case or field studies
  2. Explanatory purposes: multiple case studies, historical reporting, field studies, or ethnography
  3. Descriptive purposes: field studies, case studies, or ethnographies

Maxwell's (1996) recommendations
  1. Conceptual considerations
  2. Pragmatic considerations

Implications
  1. Qualitative research is well suited for describing, interpreting, and explaining.
  2. Qualitative research is not well suited for examining issues of prevalence, generalizability, or calibration.

---

when the study's situation requires substantial (a) data reduction, (b) clarification in the presentation of these data, and (c) expectations for new theoretical propositions or specific managerial actions. In other words, qualitative research may be the best choice when the identification of new theoretical propositions or managerial actions is deemed necessary, but the researcher is not fully knowledgeable about the details of the phenomena under immediate study.

Below, I discuss three typical approaches to deciding whether or not to use qualitative research. Miles and Huberman's (1994) recommendations have been quite influential, and I address their work at some length. In contrast, Marshall and Rossman (1995) and Maxwell (1996) both serve to reinforce Miles and Huberman's message; thus, I present their work more briefly. Table 3.1 summarizes the recommendations of all these authors.

Miles and Huberman's Four Considerations

Miles and Huberman (1994) advise researchers to address four inter-related points when they first consider qualitative research designs: local grounding, richness and holism, sustained period and causality, and lived meanings.

Local grounding. Is local grounding important? That is, do the study's site (e.g., the specific organization under study), participants (e.g., its employees or contractors), and processes (e.g., managerial decisions and organizational systems) hold intrinsic interest? For example, in high-technology firms, the decisions of chief executive officers and strategic marketing decisions are universally judged by management scholars to be worthy of empirical study because of their potential influence on large numbers of employees, if not the larger society in general. Most management scholars were both amazed and intrigued when Microsoft announced in 1996 a shift from its primary (and incredibly lucrative) focus on products involving personal computer operating systems (i.e., PC platforms) to those involving networks, with particular emphasis on Internet applications. Because of Microsoft's relative size in the industry, its products' large market shares, and its potential to define industry standards for virtually all Internet applications (and thereby affect how billions of people live their everyday lives), most organizational researchers would likely deem this business decision worthy of in-depth study. (Note that it would be quite difficult to study Microsoft's decision to shift in a context-neutral manner.)

In addition to specific decisions, some organizational processes can be understood only if their contexts are included in the analyses. For instance, a researcher may be interested in the timing of new product introductions in high-technology markets. If the researcher does not judge the particular organizational contexts in which these decision processes occur to be critical to the timing issue, he or she should consider random sampling from the larger population of interest, survey research, or commercially available primary or secondary data sources. In contrast, another researcher might be interested in Microsoft's specific decision-making processes because of its position as the world's dominant software firm. In such a case, the researcher would want to include Microsoft's leaders' personalities and the firm's highly involving company culture in any analysis. In this example, local context could not be easily ignored, and qualitative research would merit serious consideration.

Richness and holism. Is substantial depth important? That is, do descriptions that are rich, vivid, and deep hold intrinsic interest? Miles and Huberman suggest that a qualitative research report should strike the reader with a feel of "truth" about the study. It should, ideally, have a strong and long-term effect on the reader's memory. For example, organizational researchers seldom deal with events involving life and death, a worldwide audience, or long-term multimedia coverage. Yet Vaughan's (1990) case description of the *Challenger* tragedy successfully captures the richness, drama, and holism of the event. Many organizational scholars who have read Vaughan's report have likely been left with compelling feelings of sadness, amazement that the tragedy could have happened at all, and at least some admiration for the research report itself.

Sustained period and causality. In addition to the importance of contextual dependence and descriptive richness, is a longitudinal effort required? That is, should organizational or human processes be observed, monitored, or recorded over some lengthy period of time? Furthermore, the nature of qualitative research is often assumed to lend itself to *causal* inferences. For example, Zabusky spent 11 months as a participant observer at the European Space Agency, where she studied the conflicting role identities of that organization's scientists (Zabusky & Barley, 1997). In such agencies, scientists are often characterized as "problem employees" because of their desire to be members in good standing within both the academic research community and their employing organization. Using multiple methods, Zabusky verified four types of structural relationships between memberships in the academic community and the European Space Agency.

Lived meanings. Finally, are the perspectives of the people involved central to the study? That is, a defining characteristic of qualitative research is its focus on the participants' point of view. In addition to assessing and recording participants' unique perceptions, assumptions, prejudgments, presuppositions, and connections to their social worlds, qualitative research also seeks to understand how these entities are organized and structured by the participants themselves. In this way, how and why organizational members socially construct and behave within their constructed worlds should become clearer. For example, Rynes, Bretz, and Gerhart (1991) interviewed 41 graduating college seniors two times each (for a total of 82 interviews) and allowed these people to describe their recruitment experiences in their own words and from their individual perspectives. The first interview with each senior was conducted early during the recruiting process and usually soon after the subject's initial campus interview. It focused on how the individual assessed his or her initial fit and changes to that initial fit with the recruiting organization. The second interview was conducted later in the recruiting process and involved the individual's assessments of his or her site visits, job choices, and reactions to the recruiting process itself. A key element of this study was its focus on the recruits' perspective on the recruitment process.

Marshall and Rossman's Recommendations

Much like Miles and Huberman (1994), Marshall and Rossman (1995, pp. 41-43) suggest that qualitative designs are the best choice when the researcher answers yes to one or more of the following six questions:

1. Is it important for the researcher to understand the in-depth processes that operate within the organization or industry?
2. Do the research issues involve poorly understood organizational phenomena and systems?
3. Is the researcher interested in the differences between stated organizational policies and their actual implementation (e.g., strategic versus operative plans; Mintzberg, 1994)?
4. Does the researcher want to study ill-structured linkages within organizational entities?
5. Does the study involve variables that do not lend themselves to experiments for practical or ethical reasons?
6. Is the point of the study to discover new or thus far unspecified variables?

Presuming one or more affirmative answers to these questions, the study's explicit purpose then becomes the defining issue. If the study's purpose is *exploratory* in nature (e.g., to investigate poorly understood phenomena, to generate preliminary hypotheses), then the researcher should consider case or field studies. If the study's purpose is *explanatory* (e.g., to clarify causal forces, to identify operative networks), then multiple case studies, historical reporting, field surveys, or ethnography could be used. If the study's purpose is *descriptive*, field studies, case studies, or ethnographies are viable methods. If the purpose is *predictive*, qualitative research would likely be a poor choice, and so should be avoided.

Maxwell's Considerations

Conceptual considerations. Maxwell (1996) offers four conceptual considerations a researcher should keep in mind when deciding whether or not to use qualitative research. His first two conceptual considerations appear equivalent to Miles and Huberman's (1994) ideas about "lived meanings" and "local grounding":

1. Are the participants' meanings or interpretations central to the research at hand?
2. Is it important for the researcher to understand the participants' experienced context?

Maxwell's second two considerations resemble points specified by Marshall and Rossman (1995):

3. Does the researcher's interest center on the identification of unintended consequences?
4. Does the research question concern causal processes among events and actions?

One or more yes answers to the above questions suggest the viability of qualitative research. More specifically, organizational researchers often study new variables or poorly understood constructs and processes. Thus, they may find it necessary to expend substantial time and effort in clarifying the parameters of the phenomena of interest before they can make subsequent efforts to calibrate these parameters. For example, Human and Provan (1997) were interested in the network links among small manufacturing companies. Because of insufficient theory, they first conducted a qualitative study aimed at generating an initial conceptual framework. In order to calibrate their initial ideas, they conducted a quantitative survey study. When the results of both studies were analyzed, Human and Provan were able to offer several theoretical propositions grounded in empirical data. Thus, they conducted a "course-grained study" followed by a "fine-grained study" (i.e., a two-phase study).

Pragmatic considerations. In addition to conceptual issues, Maxwell offers three interrelated and pragmatic considerations that often affect researchers' decisions concerning the use of qualitative designs. First, in qualitative research the foci on local grounding, holism, longitudinal contact, and lived meanings can enhance the credibility of a study among its participants and other organizational members. Correspondingly, such a study's results are often taken as understandable, believable, and meaningful. Second, these foci and the study's perceived credibility can also enhance organizational practices. Participants and other organizational members can readily see the implications of the obtained results. The entire qualitative research process is sensitive to, if not grounded in, how participants understand and experience the phenomena under study in their everyday lives. Third, enhanced credibility and potential to improve organizational practice can enhance the likelihood of cooperation among the study's participants. In other words, they may be more apt to respond to researcher requests for information (e.g., interviews, direct observations, surveys). To the extent that one or more of these pragmatic considerations are deemed important, the desirability of qualitative research is enhanced.

Comment

Miles and Huberman (1994) correctly suggest that researchers should actively consider the use of qualitative research designs when understanding one or more of the following characteristics is particularly important to the issue at hand: (a) contextualization, (b) vivid description, (c) dynamic (and possibly causal) structuring of the organizational member's socially constructed world, and (d) the worldviews of the people under study. If emphasis on these characteristics is not clearly necessary to address the researcher's issue, the decision between qualitative versus mainstream quantitative designs cannot readily be made. The researcher may need to make the decision based on other considerations, such as personal preference, resource constraints, and the optimization of publishability of the finished report in a targeted journal. If emphasis on these characteristics is required, however, qualitative designs would appear to be preferable.

Taken as a whole, Miles and Huberman (1994), Marshall and Rossman (1995), and Maxwell (1996) suggest that qualitative research seems best suited to answering questions of description, interpretation, and explanation, and most often from the perspective of the organizational member under study. They also suggest that qualitative studies seem poorly suited to the investigation of issues of a phenomenon's prevalence, generalizability, or calibration.

In the next two sections, we turn our attention to how specific qualitative methods can serve to create new theory or theoretical propositions. It should be recognized that many other qualitative techniques can be useful in generating theory. I have chosen the particular methods described below for purposes of illustration. Nonetheless, they appear to me to be potentially useful for the exploration of many organizational research issues. First, I describe grounded theory; this is followed by a discussion of focus groups.

The final two sections of this chapter address how specific qualitative methods can serve to test hypotheses and theory. In one section, I describe case study research; in the other, the conversational interview. It should be recognized, again, that many qualitative techniques, including case studies and conversational interviews, can be useful both for generating and for testing theory (Yin, 1994). I describe case study research and the conversational interview here for purposes of illustration. In particular, these two methods appear well suited to theory testing.

Grounded Theory

According to Larsson and Lowendahl (1996), grounded theory (Glaser & Strauss, 1967; Strauss, 1987) has been the dominant qualitative method used in studies published in the organizational sciences. Moreover, my observation of the qualitative studies published in management journals since Larsson and Lowendahl's report is that this dominance continues unabated. In Chapter 2, I presented an overview of Marshall and Rossman's (1995) description of the main components of grounded theory research; the reader may (or may not) find it useful to review that part of Chapter 2 before continuing with the following discussion.

The main purpose of grounded theory studies is to generate new theory or conceptual propositions, and the main application of grounded theory techniques has been to the examination of phenomena that are not well understood. Thus, grounded theory is important to management scientists because of its (a) broad applicability to many organizational issues and situations and (b) sheer prevalence.

An underlying assumption in grounded theory is that social phenomena are complex. Correspondingly, the specific steps taken to study these complex social phenomena need to be flexible (i.e., reflexive). Thus, there can be no hard-and-fast rules about how to conduct grounded theory research. Instead, there are only general guidelines, which are presented below. In the following subsections, I describe grounded theory through (a) three defining process issues, (b) a generic process, and (c) its main components.

Three Defining Processes

Ongoing interpretations. Because the creation of theory about complex social and organizational phenomena is the intended outcome, grounded theory methodology requires that data be interpreted on a continual and evolving basis. That is, the researcher must continually revisit and revise his or her interpretations. Given new information, changes in the framing of and intensive debate on the issue at hand should follow. *Rich description, conceptual density,* and *microscopic and intensive examination* are all phrases commonly used in characterizing grounded theory data and their treatment. Overall, the spirit of ongoing interpretations is to examine the data from all possible perspectives under conditions of rigorous debate and intellectually honest skepticism.

Experiential data. In conducting ongoing interpretations, the researcher brings his or her own experiences to bear on the empirical data. Since Glaser and Strauss (1967) published their defining work, however, some disagreement on the role of personal experience has emerged (Locke, 1996). On the one hand, Strauss (1987) argues that the grounded theory approach requires researchers to apply actively any and all prior knowledge and insight while conducting ongoing interpretations. If they do otherwise, they risk overlooking possible interpretations. On the other hand, Glaser (1992) argues for a more passive role on the part of researchers. He asserts that they should be limited to interpreting what is clearly evident in the data; that is, interpretations should derive primarily from the data themselves. If they do otherwise, they risk imposing on the data too many of their own personal biases. Thus, this disagreement involves the extent to which a researcher "imposes interpretations on" versus "reads existing interpretations from" the data. To date, there has been no resolution to this issue; the researcher's involvement remains a matter of personal comfort.

Induction, deduction, and verification. Because new theory is the intended outcome, grounded theory is often assumed, incorrectly, to be an exercise in inductive reasoning only. In reality, it is much more. The grounded theory process requires that all ideas, speculations, and hypotheses, which are derived from empirical data, be considered tentative. Much as in normal science (Kuhn, 1996), these preliminary notions must then be subjected to subsequent empirical testing against additional data, which is a deductive exercise. Ideally, these notions should be (a) inductively derived, (b) deductively tested, (c) inductively or deductively revised, and (d) retested against additional empirical data.

Generic Processes

As suggested, the spirit of grounded theory is that of a continuous and interrelated process of hypothesis generation, data collection, empirical testing, and theory (or concept) revision about some organizational phenomenon. Moreover, this spirit involves conceptual movement from speculation to formal theorizing. It cannot be overemphasized that, when using this technique, the researcher must stay data based and tightly connected to the empirical world.

Eight generic steps can be distinguished in the grounded theory approach. First, the researcher generates tentative ideas, questions, and concepts about some organizational phenomenon of interest. Second, the researcher suggests some potential underlying concepts for this organizational phenomenon and their linkages (it is this second step that constitutes the beginning of "conceptually dense theory"—i.e., theory creation). Third, the researcher tests these preliminary linkages against empirical data. Fourth, the researcher strives continually to relate these concepts to the objective world. (The third and fourth steps start the process of preliminary theory testing.) Fifth, the researcher strives to integrate, simplify, and reduce the central concepts and their inter-relationships (this is the onset of theory refinement). Sixth, the researcher engages in the production of "theoretical memos" (described below) while conducting the mechanical procedures of empirical testing, revision, and retesting of concepts. Seventh, the researcher conducts data collection, coding, and interpretation in a dynamic and reciprocal manner; this often involves the return to earlier steps. Eighth, the researcher writes the research report; this is part of the creative process itself, not merely a detached, mechanical exercise.

Main Components

Concept-indicator model. Through the generic processes described above, grounded theory research results in the identification of (a) one or more core concepts, (b) the empirical indicators of these core concepts, and (c) the conceptual and empirical relationships among these core concepts and their manifest indicators. More operationally, the researcher spends a great deal of time and effort (a) creating categories (i.e., concepts) that explain or underlie the empirical data, (b) coding empirical indicators into these categories, and (c) collecting sequential data sets with which to test and improve the fit of these empirical indicators. Metaphorically, the grounded theory researcher is conducting a qualitative *factor analysis.*

Data collection. Although data usually come from interviews or participant observations, information can also be gleaned from published documents (e.g., company handbooks) and private documents (e.g., personal journals, memos). Most important, however, data collection must be directed. Except under conditions of virtual ignorance, the type and nature of the collected data should be determined by a particular hypothesis or revision to a hypothesis. It is rarely the case that a researcher collects data without having some core category in mind, except perhaps at the very beginning of a study.

Coding. Coding is the actual process through which the data (i.e., the empirical indicators) are organized into some theoretically meaningful structure. The assignment of empirical indicators to their underlying factors is usually done in one of three ways: through open coding, axial coding, or selective coding.

Open coding refers to an unrestricted mode in which the researcher identifies the "naturally occurring" categories depicted by the data themselves. In other words, the researcher creates as many categories as needed in order to organize, explain, and assign the empirical data to these categories in a coherent fashion. Recall the simple example from Chapter 2 in which each datum is recorded on a 3-by-5 card. A datum could be a behavioral observation, a participant's verbal comment, or a researcher's interpretation. Conceptual categories (or theoretical organization) could be represented by the physical arrangement of these cards in piles on a tabletop. Open coding could be accomplished through the creation of as many piles of cards as are needed to achieve a coherent structure. Note, however, that this unstructured approach can quickly become unwieldy and overly complex. As such, its most useful application may be at the very beginning of the coding process.

Axial coding refers to the assignment of empirical indicators to one category at a time. First, the researcher proposes several categories. Second, the researcher selects a single category and then judges all the data as to whether or not they fit within that selected category. The researcher then selects another category and judges all the remaining data in relation to that category. This process is repeated until all data have been evaluated against all categories and classified, each datum in a single category. Ideally, all data would clearly fit into the existing categories. Returning to the simple example involving 3-by-5 cards, each category title could be written on an individual card. The researcher would then select a single title card and judge each data card for its fit within that category. After the researcher has judged all the data cards against this first category, he or she would select a second title card and judge all the remaining data cards for fit within this second category. The process would be repeated until each of the data cards has been judged to fit within one, and only one, category. Most often, axial coding is done later in a study, usually after the researcher has achieved some confidence as to the data's basic structure.

Selective coding refers to the imposition of an ordering on the categories' importance. First, the researcher proposes several categories. Second, the researcher orders the categories according to their potential to have data fit within them. Third, the researcher selects the most powerful (or important) category and judges all the data for their fit within that selected category. Fourth, the researcher selects the next most important category and judges all data for their fit within it. This process is repeated with each category until all the data have been categorized, ideally with each datum falling into one and only one category.

Core categories. Throughout the process of grounded theory research, identification of the most important, or *core*, categories is of the utmost concern. Strauss (1987) offers six guidelines for identifying core categories. First, the category must be central. A core category should be conceptually related to (or ideally explain) as many other categories and their properties as possible. Second, the category must explain a substantial amount of the data. As many empirical indicators should be judged to fit into that category as possible. Third, connections between a core and other categories should not be forced onto the data—they should occur "naturally." Fourth, the implications of a core category to a larger theory should be quite evident (this also should not be a forced connection). Fifth, the core category's fit with the data should improve across subsequent waves of data collection. Sixth, a core category should maximize variance. More specifically, it should fit with as many patterns found in the data as possible. Returning to the factor analysis metaphor, the grounded theory researcher should seek robust, general factors and ignore more limited specific factors.

Theoretical sampling. As hypotheses are generated, evaluated, revised, and reevaluated, the researcher must collect data in order to conduct these sequential tests. *Theoretical sampling* is the label applied to the specific reasons a revised hypothesis must be tested. Theoretical sampling provides the explanation for why data are collected from particular individuals, groups, populations, events, activities, or other such entities. It constitutes the conceptual *purpose* for gathering the next wave of data. The researcher samples in order to test revised hypotheses; the more rigorous the test, the better the sampling.

Theoretical saturation. The sequential process of hypothesis, data collection, and testing must have an end point. Specifically, the process stops when further hypothesizing, revising, and data collection are judged unlikely to lead to additional understanding—in other words, additional data would produce minimal learning. The term *theoretical saturation* describes such a stopping point. Returning to the simple example with the 3-by-5 cards, theoretical saturation has been achieved when further rearrangement of the card piles—and therefore the emergent conceptual structure—produces no further insight, knowledge, or learning.

Theoretical memos. At each step of the grounded theory process, each member of the research team should record his or her alternative hypotheses, speculations, and corresponding explanations in a series of memos written to the larger research team. These memos should then serve as the basis for subsequent discussion, debate, and interpretation. Over time, the content of these memos should move toward a coherent theory or set of conceptual propositions. Thus, theoretical memos can represent the field data, its analytic evolution, and a historical record of the study itself.

Comment

Grounded theory is a long-term, labor-intensive, and time-consuming process. It requires multiple waves of data collection, with each wave of data based on theoretical sampling. In addition, the iterative process should continue until theoretical saturation is achieved. Given all this, researchers should avoid grounded theory approaches unless they can commit substantial resources to a study. Under most circumstances, doctoral students doing dissertation work (and perhaps their professor advisers as well) would be well-advised to evaluate the resource implications quite carefully before committing to grounded theory research.

It might be noted that organizational researchers often claim to take a "grounded theory orientation" (Larsson & Lowendahl, 1996). However, grounded theory as defined by Glaser and Strauss (1967) appears to be conducted rarely by organizational researchers (Locke, 1996). Because there are no hard-and-fast rules for grounded theory research, it is difficult to say whether the method has been misapplied. Nonetheless, Larsson and Lowendahl's (1996) disturbing observation that the grounded theory label is used more often for purposes of conceptual justification (to journal reviewers) than for accurate description appears correct.

Focus Groups

Like grounded theory research, focus groups appear well suited to the generation of theory. Morgan (1997) notes that "the hallmark of focus groups is their explicit use of group interaction to produce data and insights that would be less accessible without the interaction found in a group" (p. 2). In other words, focus groups generate data that are (a) related to the themes imposed by a researcher and (b) enriched by the group's interactive discussion.

The mechanics of the focus group are simple: A small group of individuals (e.g., 4-12) from a theoretically meaningful population (e.g., organizational members, product consumers, graduating college seniors) are assembled and asked to respond to a series of questions. These questions are intended to prompt an active conversation among group members, and it is through such discussion that in-depth information can be gathered along the theoretical or conceptual themes imposed by the researcher. (Focus groups are described briefly in this section; additional detail on how to conduct focus groups is provided in Chapter 4.) For example, Maurer, Howe, and Lee (1992) studied whether graduating engineering students respond to organizational recruitment efforts as product consumers respond to sales processes. They conducted four focus groups at three different universities with small groups of engineering seniors who were about to undergo the organizational recruitment process. With Maurer serving as the focus group facilitator, group discussion identified the nature of the students' motives and attitudes along the theme (or metaphor) of a product consumer. These data led Maurer et al. to formulate a preliminary understanding and some hypotheses, which they subsequently tested quantitatively (i.e., this was a two-phase design). More specifically, the data allowed the researchers to develop a questionnaire survey that they later administered to a large nationwide sample of graduating engineering students, the data from which they then analyzed quantitatively.

Common Uses

Morgan (1997) identifies at least four particular research functions for focus groups. These are discussed in turn below.

Self-contained focus groups. A common assumption among many researchers is that focus groups can serve only as an antecedent step to other research methods. However, focus groups can also be self-contained entities useful in the study of individual- and group-level variables. By conducting one or more focus groups, a researcher can collect data on individuals' opinions, attitudes, and self-reported behaviors. More important, the interactive discussions that take place in focus groups—in which members share and compare their experiences, resulting in potentially powerful social facilitation—can provide researchers with substantial insight into group-level phenomena.

Focus groups and interviews. Given the prevalence of interviewing in qualitative research, the connection between focus groups and interviews may be self-evident. Data from focus groups can be quite valuable to interview studies in at least three ways. First, focus group discussions can yield the topics around which specific interview questions are written. For example, the themes a focus group is gathered to discuss might represent the researcher's best ideas about what topics to cover in a subsequent interview-based study. In the focus group itself, discussion on these themes may lead to the identification of specific subtopics, potential questions, or entirely new topics. Thus, focus group data can serve as the basis for a subsequent study's actual interview questions. Second, focus groups can provide information about whom to interview and the potential value of different research sites. For instance, the researcher might have a clear idea of what to ask, but may be uncertain about which individuals he or she should interview. Through one or more focus groups, key persons, groups, and situations may be readily identified. Third, focus groups can be valuable after a researcher has completed the substantive data collection and analysis in a qualitative (or quantitative) study. In particular, focus groups can serve as a mechanism for clarifying ambiguous or poorly understood information uncovered during a study's interviews. For example, the researcher might reassemble the original focus group or assemble an entirely new focus group and ask the members to make further sense of an earlier interview study's data.

Focus groups and participant observation studies. Just as they often are valuable for interview studies, focus groups can be valuable to participant observation studies in at least two ways. Before a study begins, conducting one or more focus groups can serve as a researcher's initial exposure to a field location. The focus group discussions can introduce the researcher to the organization's culture, the range of its members' worldviews, and key individuals within the field setting. In a sense, conducting such focus groups can sensitize the researcher to what to expect. After a study's data collection and analyses are presumed completed, the results can also be fed back through focus groups to the study's participants and other organizational members, for what Marshall and Rossman (1995) call "member checks." Such feedback can stimulate focus group discussion that may provide the researcher with additional insight into the reasonableness, correctness, and validity of his or her interpretations.

Focus groups and surveys and experiments. As in Maurer et al.'s (1992) work, focus groups can aid in the development of questionnaires at the outset of a study. They can help the researcher to identify domains of interest, specify their content, and clarify context-specific wording of questions. After a survey or an experiment is completed, focus groups can also be valuable for clarifying the study's results. The researcher can use the discussion of one or more focus groups to explore the survey or experimental results for likely meanings and questions that naturally follow from the perspective of organizational members.

Strengths and Weaknesses

Like all research techniques, focus groups have certain strengths and weaknesses. The greatest strength of the focus group may be its efficiency. A focus group can quickly elicit a substantial amount of information on a particular topic. Moreover, the interactive nature of the focus group allows for the immediate input of several persons. Thus, a researcher can readily collect and evaluate data and modify hypotheses based on the interaction among group members.

A weakness of the focus group is that it is limited to verbal descriptions and within-group interactions. It does not allow the researcher to gain firsthand knowledge of the described opinions, attitudes, and behaviors in their real-world contexts. Moreover, the group nature of this research technique means that the time available for any individual member to express his or her opinions or attitudes or to describe associ- ated behaviors is rather short. Thus, a focus group may not produce the depth or richness of information that may be gathered using other qualitative techniques.

Comment

Although the focus group can constitute a self-contained research technique (Morgan, 1997), this seems an unlikely use of the technique by organizational scientists. Instead, the focus group is more valuable as a supplemental technique that serves to enhance and enrich the data collected using another qualitative or quantitative technique. Organiza- tional researchers have not commonly employed focus groups in their studies. Nonetheless, they might be well-advised to consider the use of focus group methods as part of their qualitative research efforts, particu- larly in dominant-less dominant designs and in the generation of new theory (described in Chapter 1).

Case Study Research

According to Larsson and Lowendahl (1996), Yin's (1994) case study research method has been the qualitative method mentioned second most often in studies published in the organizational sciences. Although its main purpose in the management literature has been to generate new theory, Yin argues that case study research lends itself to the testing of existing theory as well. In particular, he suggests that case study research is best suited to the examination of why and how contemporary, real-life (organizational) phenomena occur, but under conditions where re- searchers have minimal control.

Case study research addresses many of the questions traditionally answered by laboratory or field experiments. The major difference, of course, is that case study research does not (and cannot) require con- trol and manipulation of variables. In addition, many qualitative re- searchers, myself included, believe that the case study's in-depth nature and emphasis on situationally embedded processes justify some level of causal inference.

Below, I provide a detailed description of an application of the case study method. I then discuss the main components of case study research, using the preceding application purposes of illustration. At the outset, it important to note that, as in much of the qualitative research domain, there are no hard-and-fast rules governing case study research. Only general guidelines can be offered. (A general description is presented in this section; for additional technical details on how to conduct case study research, see Chapter 4.)

The Tested Theory

The unfolding model of voluntary turnover (Lee & Mitchell, 1994) proposes that employees quit organizations through four prototypical decision paths. In three of these paths, the quitting process is initiated by a "shock to the system." This shock is theorized to be a jarring, external-to-the-person event that can be characterized as (a) expected or unexpected; (b) good, neutral, or bad; and (c) involving individual, job, or organizational events. Furthermore, the four prototypical decision paths vary in the amount of psychological deliberation involved on the part of the employee. Deliberation can vary from a quick judgment, unencumbered by multiple characteristics, to a highly rational analysis of costs and benefits.

In decision path 1, a shock is theorized to elicit a memory probe for a recollection of a highly similar shock, situation, and response (i.e., a scripted action plan), which can originate from prior experiences or vicarious learning. If an action plan is recalled from memory, the response of staying or quitting is enacted. If such a plan is not recalled, another decision path is initiated. Thus, the essential features of decision path 1 are shock and enactment of a preexisting action plan. For example, a female employee may have made a plan that when she becomes pregnant with her first child, she will stay home for a few years to care for the child (i.e., her scripted action plan). When pregnancy actually occurs (i.e., the shock), the preexisting action plan is engaged, and the woman quits her job. (Note that a shock need not be negative or unexpected.)

In decision path 2, a shock prompts an individual to assess how much he or she wants to *remain* with the current organization. This assessment occurs in the absence of a specific job alternative and results in the binary outcome of staying or leaving. Two psychological mechanisms are theorized. First, the shock and accompanying situation are judged against the individual's personal values, goals, and plans toward attainment of those goals. Second, a judgment of incompatibility among the shock, the situation, and the person's values, goals, and goal plans leads to the person's quitting. In contrast, a judgment of compatibility leads to his or her staying. Thus, the essential features of decision path 2 are shock and judgments of fit. For example, a woman is bypassed for a promotion (i.e., a shock). As a result, she may feel that her career has been so seriously damaged (incompatibility between the shock and her career goals) that she can no longer work for the organization. She then quits with no particular alternative in mind.

In decision path 3, a shock prompts an employee to assess how much he or she wants to *leave* the current organization. Unlike decision path 2, this assessment occurs in the presence a specific job alternative and results in a three-step decision process. First, the shock, the situation, and the individual's values, goals, and goal plans are judged for compatibility. A judgment of compatibility results in the person's staying. A judgment of incompatibility results in some level of disaffection, and it is this disaffection that initiates a search for alternatives. Second, the located alternatives are judged for compatibility with the individual's values, goals, and goal plans. A judgment of incompatibility results in deletion of the alternative from further consideration. A judgment of compatibility results in the decision to subject that surviving alternative to further scrutiny. Third, the surviving alternatives are subjected to detailed and rational analysis of costs and benefits. The option that maximizes the individual's preferences is ultimately selected. Thus, the essential features of decision path 3 are shock, compatibility judgments, disaffection, job search, evaluation, and job offers in hand.

In decision path 4, no shock is involved. Instead, organizational life is seen as ongoing, with few distinguishing demarcations. Over time, the employee, the organization, or both can change so that they grow apart and the individual's values, goals, and goal plans no longer fit with what the organization can offer. Note that this change, evaluation, and realization are gradual. At some point, the employee may experience so much job dissatisfaction that he or she simply quits. Alternatively, the dissatisfaction may prompt the employee to search for a better job and then leave.

An Empirical Case Study Test of the Unfolding Model

Given its complexity and dynamic nature, the unfolding model does not readily lend itself to standard experimental or survey research. Experimentation seems infeasible because the demands for control and manipulation of variables are too great. Likewise, a survey study seems infeasible because the questionnaire would need to be extraordinarily complex. More pragmatically, finding a host organization in which to conduct such an experiment or a survey appears virtually impossible.

Beyond constraints, however, my colleagues and I judged that a valid test of the unfolding model needed to account for at least three of the theory's inherent characteristics (Lee, Mitchell, Wise, & Fireman, 1996). First, the theory specifies the interactive effects of individual and situational characteristics. Whereas judgments about personal values, goals, and goal plans are individual-specific variables, for instance, shocks and the circumstances in which they occur are situational variables. Separation of individual variables from situational characteristics would result in an invalid test of the unfolding model itself. A valid test of the unfolding model must include both types of variables. In the jargon of qualitative research, local grounding, richness, and holism are essential (Miles & Huberman, 1994).

Second, the unfolding model is dynamic in nature. In each decision path, antecedents and consequences are specified. For example, shocks precede action in decision paths 1, 2, and 3. A valid test of the unfolding model must allow for these processes to develop over time (hence the term *unfolding*). In the absence of a longitudinal design, the unfolding model could not be assessed validly. In the jargon of qualitative research, a sustained period and causal inference are required (Miles & Huberman, 1994).

Third, the decision path's essential features are defined from the perspective of the organizational member. Shocks, compatibility judgments, and evaluations, for instance, are from the employee's point of view. Thus, as in much of the qualitative research domain, a valid test of the unfolding model must take the participant's viewpoint. In the jargon of qualitative research, lived experience is theoretically mandated (Miles & Huberman, 1994).

When we considered these constraints and inherent characteristics together, we chose case study research to assess why and how employees quit their organizations. We identified 44 nurses who had recently quit their jobs and conducted semistructured and in-depth interviews with them to learn about their quitting experiences. In addition to eliciting general descriptions of their situations and experiences, we used probing follow-up questions to assess whether the essential features of each decision path occurred or—equally important—did not occur as theorized. Thus, these nurses themselves told us whether the hypothesized pattern of essential features occurred (or did not occur) in their own quitting experiences.

Yin (1994) also advises case study researchers to include quantitative analysis when appropriate. Thus, we supplemented our qualitative analysis with log linear modeling and logistic regressions (i.e., a two-phase study). These qualitative analyses yielded judgments about whether the process variables (i.e., the essential features) occurred or did not occur as theorized by the unfolding model. In essence (and also in Kvale's, 1996, terms), we studied the nature and changes in categorical states. In contrast, the quantitative analyses yielded statistical estimates for the likelihood of the occurrences of these categorical states. Moreover, these methods of categorical data analysis allowed for the identification of statistical associations between the onset of each decision path and its theorized characteristics. Again in Kvale's (1996) terms, calibration of these likelihoods was empirically estimated.

Main Components

Case study research has five primary components: (a) research questions, (b) theoretical propositions, (c) units of analysis, (d) the logic linking data to these theoretical propositions, and (e) the criteria for evaluating these propositions. Component d concerns a study's specific techniques; these techniques are covered in Chapters 4 and 5. Component e concerns the study's construct- and criterion-related validity; these issues are discussed in Chapter 7. Below, I discuss components a, b, and c, using the Lee et al. (1996) study as a running example.

Research Questions

Like experimental research, case study research tends to focus on how and why organizational phenomena occur. In the Lee et al. study, the main hypotheses focused on whether each decision path's essential features occurred or did not occur as theoretically predicted. That is, each decision path had a unique sequence for the occurrence and nonoccurrence of essential features. In decision path 1, for example, a shock occurs and scripted behavior follows. In addition to these specific essential features, the unfolding model holds that search for and evaluation of alternatives do not occur in decision path 1. From the interviewees' verbal reports, each decision path's essential features could be judged to have occurred (or not to have occurred) as theoretically expected. Note that these reports also allow assessment of individual and contextual variables as well as the dynamic processes these variables follow over time.

Because of its in-depth nature and labor-intensive requirements, case study research usually involves few cases. Issues of prevalence most often assume secondary roles. Given the unusually high number of cases ($N = 44$) in the Lee et al. (1996) study, however, we conducted cross-case analyses. In addition to conducting qualitative analyses within cases, we conducted log linear modeling and logistic regression between cases as well. In our secondary hypotheses, for example, we estimated the statistical associations between the occurrence of particular decision paths (e.g., path 2) and their unique characteristics (e.g., negative shocks).

Theoretical Propositions

As in quantitative research in general, and experiments in particular, the tested theory guides the study's design and execution. In a deductive manner, the tested theory should clarify the specific research questions asked, variables and interactions assessed, and nature of the analysis. In the Lee et al. study, the unfolding model specified the occurrence and nonoccurrence of essential features for each decision path. Furthermore, the model specified the content and nature of these variables. As a result, the study's overall, master plan (or "protocol," in Yin's, 1994, terms) and its research questions, expectations for the kinds of data to collect, and particular analytic techniques were more readily specified during the study's planning phase. Without doubt, this clarity greatly facilitated the study's execution.

Unit of Analysis

A study's unit of analysis is the phenomenon under study. Although this appears to be straightforward, units of analyses can be deceiving in case study research. Because of this methodology's emphasis on real-world and natural contexts, attempts to isolate the (potential) phenomenon of interest from its context can quickly become muddled. Is the researcher interested in a particular decision (e.g., to quit, to enter a given product market), its enactment (e.g., actual quitting, actual product entry into that market), the people who make that decision (e.g., employees, marketing managers, marketing teams), the circumstances surrounding the decision (e.g., the employee's career stage, the market and firm pressures to act), or all of these categories in combination?

With theory generation, the researcher's decision about the unit of analysis can be made difficult, in part because one purpose of the study itself is to determine the most meaningful unit. With theory testing, the researcher's decisions about the unit of analysis are usually more apparent, because the theory itself should define the meaningful unit. Even in research aimed at theory testing, however, there is still room for ambiguity. The unfolding model, for instance, seeks to describe the phenomenon of individuals' quitting organizations through four prototypical decision paths (Lee & Mitchell, 1994). In our subsequent test of the model, my colleagues and I decided that the individual employee was the relevant unit (Lee et al., 1996). Alternatively, an argument can easily be made that the unfolding model focuses more on the decision to leave and less on the act of quitting itself. Instead of asking about the act of quitting, a test of the unfolding model could legitimately ask about the individuals' decisions to leave or to stay. Thus, there is some ambiguity whether the unfolding model is a theory about quitting or a theory about staying. Depending upon one's point of view, the unit of analysis could be (a) the act of quitting, (b) the act of staying, (c) the decision to leave, (d) the decision to stay, or (e) all of these phenomena together.

Comment

My expectation is that an increasing number of articles reporting case study research will appear in the management literature over the next decade. Indeed, I would welcome such a trend. My expectation has two bases. First, the in-depth data and local contextualization of case study research allow for stronger causal inferences than are typically allowed by correlational field studies. It should be noted that such the causal inferences from case study research are likely to be weaker than those based on *true randomized experiments* (but not necessarily those based primarily on random assignment of treatments to subjects). (I am omitting those field studies that utilize structural equation modeling, which also allows for some degree of causal inference.) Because of this stronger basis (both potential and actual) for causal inferences, case study research may be well-suited to the exploration of those organizational questions and situations that do not lend themselves to traditional experimental designs. Simply put, case study research is another potentially useful tool that may lend itself to causal inference. As such, it should be welcomed by organizational researchers.

Second, case study research is usually far less disruptive to organizations than are formal field experiments. Because the method typically involves interviewing individual employees or observing their behavior, albeit in their organizational context, case study research can often appear less intrusive (and disruptive) than most field-based survey studies or experiments. Note that I am referring to *appearances*, and not necessarily to actual intrusion. Nonetheless, the likelihood of individual and organizational cooperation can be enhanced. Given the common difficulty in obtaining such field cooperation, facilitating access to data should also appeal to empirical researchers.

Conversational Interviews

Interview Structure

Interviews can range in style from completely structured to completely unstructured. Semistructured interviews fall between the end points in this range. Below, I offer brief descriptions of structured, unstructured, and semistructured interviews.

Completely structured interviews. Completely structured interviews are essentially verbally conducted questionnaires that include fixed response options. Most often, questions are read aloud to the interviewee and responses are recorded by the interviewer. In addition to verbalizing the survey items, the interviewer's responsibilities include ensuring that the interviewee understands the questions and that responses are not haphazardly given. Some skill is required on the part of the interviewer, of course, but this kind of interviewing is not considered demanding. Overall, completely structured interviews have a mechanical and directed feel about them. They are often useful, for instance, when respondents do not have sufficient verbal skills or tolerance for written materials to undertake less structured interviews.

Completely unstructured interviews. Completely unstructured interviews are ad hoc in nature. The interviewer typically has an overarching topic, but, unlike in the structured interview, there tend not to be general themes, targeted issues, or specific questions planned a priori. Instead, themes, issues, and questions emerge from the ongoing interaction between interviewer and interviewee. Moreover, the interviewer is free to pursue matters deemed appropriate given the immediate discourse. The interviewer's primary responsibilities are (a) to facilitate conversation along lines of the overarching topic, (b) to detect themes related to the overarching topic from the interview's discourse, (c) to probe for deeper answers and meanings, (d) to identify completely new topics that relate to the original topic, and (e) to probe these new topics as well. Needless to say, an interviewer requires strong skills to conduct unstructured interviews. Overall, unstructured interviews have a free-flowing and open flavor. Such interviews are often useful, for example, when a study's data are reflexively interpreted (see Chapter 2).

Semistructured interviews. Semistructured interviews represent a compromise between structured and unstructured formats. Semistructured interviews usually have an overarching topic, general themes, targeted issues, and specific questions, with a predetermined sequence for their occurrence. As in the unstructured interview, but unlike the structured format, the interviewer is free to pursue matters as circumstances dictate. In the Lee et al. study, for example, interviewers entered with a predetermined interview schedule (i.e., set of themes, targeted issues, and specific questions) and were instructed to (and did) freely pursue emergent topics and themes and to probe more deeply than the initial planned questions. Unlike the structured interview, but as in the unstructured format, the semistructured interview requires strong interviewer skills. Overall, the semistructured interview should maintain a balance between a free-flowing and a directed conversation.

Generic Conversational Interviews

In qualitative research, the conversational interview is implemented in a semistructured format. However, it clearly falls toward the unstructured, as opposed to the structured, end of the continuum. In the conversational interview, the interviewer pursues predetermined themes and is free to pursue and probe for additional meaning. Although most useful in generating theory, conversational interviews can also effectively lend themselves to testing theory. (Below, I provide a brief description of the conversational interview; for additional details on how to conduct such interviews, see Chapter 4.)

The overarching topic of the interview is the theory of interest. In a deductive fashion, the researcher derives predetermined themes and issues from the theory of interest, and develops at least some specific questions before interviewing begins. The interviewer is instructed to pursue theoretical details, subtleties, and inconsistencies within and across the predetermined themes (e.g., pattern matching, which is described in Chapter 4). Using the responses to the predetermined and follow-up questions, the researcher can make judgments about the theory's corroboration or falsification based on whether enough of the theory was tested (i.e., adequate coverage of the theory's conceptual domain) and on the nature and extent of the identified theoretical inconsistencies.

For example, in the Lee et al. (1996) study, we obtained self-reports through semistructured interviews with participants on the expected occurrence and nonoccurrence of the decision paths' essential features. We inferred theoretical corroboration when essential features occurred and did not occur as predicted by the unfolding model. We inferred theoretical falsification when (a) essential features occurred but were not so predicted and (b) essential features did not occur but were so expected.

Kvale (1996) suggests that the qualitative research interview has 12 defining characteristics; these characteristics can be adapted and applied to the conversational interview. First, the theory's focal concepts and topics (i.e., its conceptual domain) should reflect the everyday experiences of the interviewee. Second, the interviewer's role is to register and interpret the meaning of what is said and how it is said. Central themes and deeper meanings from the interviewee might be sought, for example. Third, qualitative, as opposed to quantitative, knowledge of the interviewee's world is sought. That is, the researcher is typically interested in issues of kind and not of degree. Fourth, as in other qualitative research, the study seeks rich and nuanced descriptions of the interviewee's world. Fifth, descriptions of specific situations and action sequences are elicited—general opinions are usually not of interest. Sixth, the interview's flavor (or feel) should be one of openness to unexpected phenomena. Such openness, however, does not preclude preexisting categories and interpretative schemes. Seventh, the conversational interview focuses on particular themes. It is, however, neither strictly structured with standardized questions nor entirely "nondirective." Eighth, it is to be expected that the interviewee's statements can be ambiguous, reflecting the contradictions in his or her experienced world. Ninth, it should be recognized that the conversational interview itself can produce changes in the interviewee's interpretation, descriptions, or themes of his or her lived world. Tenth, the interviewer's skills matter—different interviewers can elicit different statements on the same themes owing to individual sensitivity, knowledge, and insight. Eleventh, the conversational interview is inherently interpersonal. Thus, the interviewer must be prepared to deal with strong emotional reactions. In the Lee et al. study, for example, one nurse began crying profusely when she recounted her quitting experience. Finally, a well-conducted interview should be a positive experience for the interviewee.

Comment

The reader should not lose sight of the fact that qualitative research has few hard-and-fast rules. Typically, only guidelines can be provided. Nonetheless, qualitative research may be well suited to the pursuit of questions of description, interpretation, and explanation. In contrast, qualitative research may *not* be well suited to the examination of questions of prevalence, generalizability, and calibration. In this chapter, I have described grounded theory and focus group research as well suited to the generation of theory, if judged appropriate for particular research and analytic situations. Similarly, I have described case study research and conversational interviews as well suited to the testing (or falsification) of theory.

In Chapter 4, numerous specific tactics for data collection and analysis are presented. In particular, a more "how-to" orientation is evident in

Chapter 4 than in other chapters in this volume. I believe that qualitative researchers should seek to create hybrid applications by combining various tactics. Thus, the reader should approach the following chapter with an idea of how these specific tactics might be combined in his or her own research.

Specific Techniques for Focus Groups, Case Study Research, and Conversational Interviews

More than the others, this chapter (along with Chapters 5 and 6) takes a "how-to" approach in describing techniques for data collection and analysis. This chapter presents specific techniques associated with focus groups, case study research, and conversational interviews (more general issues about the overall design of these methods have been discussed in Chapters 2 and 3). Organizational examples are provided throughout this chapter, and the author recommends that researchers strive to apply multiple techniques within their studies.

Miles and Huberman's influential book *Qualitative Data Analysis* (1994) may be the best single compendium available of specific techniques for qualitative data collection, analysis, and display. Researchers should consult that volume early on in the design or start-up phase of virtually any qualitative study. Whereas a book-length work allows for coverage of a substantial number of techniques, a chapter on techniques requires decisions about what to include and what to omit. Thus, I am omitting here (and in Chapter 5) the techniques associated with grounded theory research, for two reasons. First, organizational

TABLE 4.1 Issues Involved in Focus Group Techniques

Planning focus groups
  1. Ethical issues
  2. Budget constraints
  3. Selection of participants
  4. Group structure
  5. Group size and discussion quality
  6. Number of focus groups
  7. Criteria for evaluation

Conducting focus groups
  1. Introducing the focus group
  2. Beginning discussion
  3. Substantive discussion

Data coding and analysis
  1. Frequency counts and categorical data analysis
  2. Feedback

---

researchers have treated grounded theory more as a general approach to qualitative research (Larsson & Lowendahl, 1996) than as a particular set of techniques, which was initially the case (Glaser, 1992; Glaser & Strauss, 1967; Locke, 1996; Strauss, 1987). Thus, its application usually involves a subset of the techniques described in Chapters 4 and 5. Second, grounded theory has received substantial coverage in Chapters 2 and 3, so additional coverage here would be redundant. In Chapters 2 and 3, I have discussed the larger issues of research design for focus groups (Morgan, 1997), case study research (Yin, 1994), and conversational interviews (Kvale, 1996); below, I present more technical details related to these topics. More so than other chapters in this volume, this chapter (along with Chapters 5 and 6) takes a "how-to" orientation.

Focus Group Techniques

Planning Focus Groups

Table 4.1 provides an overview of the issues involved in the use of focus group techniques. As is true of many research techniques, the appearance of focus group research can be misleading. To many people, focus groups appear to be simply small collections of individuals who sit and chat casually about assigned topics. In reality, focus groups are far more complicated. Researchers need to make several important decisions before they can conduct their first focus groups. The issues and decisions that they must address are discussed below. (Much of what follows is derived from the work of Morgan, 1997.)

Ethical issues. Almost always, focus groups are video- or audiotaped. When taping is not feasible (e.g., the host organization prohibits it), the researcher must take extensive field notes on the group discussion. Typically, participants and host organizations are informed that any video or audio recordings made will be used for research purposes only. Interestingly, such vague statements usually satisfy most participants. As a result, perhaps, many academic researchers overlook or do not seriously consider who might eventually see (or hear) these tapes. More often than not, these tapes eventually come to sit on book shelves or in file cabinets. Nonetheless, they often contain material that is potentially embarrassing to participants or the host organizations. Thus, it is strongly recommended that the researcher decide during the planning stage (a) who is likely to see the tapes (or field notes), (b) how long these tapes (or notes) will be kept before they are destroyed, and (c) whether these decisions will be disclosed to potential participants and host organizations prior to an actual focus group.

Budgetary constraints. Of course, all research operates under some budgetary constraints. These tend to be more restrictive for basic academic research, for instance, than for applied market research. It can be critical to a focus group's success for the researcher to decide (or be informed) early on during the planning process how much money is available. For example, should the participants be paid a "market rate" for their time, or should each receive a token sum simply to convey appreciation? It is not uncommon for consulting market researchers to pay each participant in a focus group $50 to $100. In basic academic research, however, it is more common to use unpaid volunteers, which is what Maurer, Howe, and Lee (1992) did, or to pay each participant a nominal amount (e.g., $5 to $20). In addition, it is often necessary to conduct focus groups at different geographic locations. Traveling to these locations can involve airfare, lodging, car rentals, and meals. Across several locations, expenses can quickly mount.

Selection of participants. As Morgan (1995) notes, recruitment of participants can be quite difficult, if not the most common problem in focus group research. Thus, availability often drives who participates in focus groups. Three recommendations can be offered on the selection of participants. First, to the extent possible, the selection of participants should be based on theoretical sampling (discussed in Chapter 3) rather than random sampling. In other words, researchers should strive to minimize identifiable forms of bias rather than to maximize statistical generalizability. It may be an understatement to say that random selection of participants would be difficult to achieve. Second, and again to the extent possible, participants should be relatively *homogeneous* along a theoretically meaningful dimension (e.g., age, sex, socioeconomic status) but *heterogeneous* across focus groups (e.g., older versus younger, male versus female, higher versus lower status). The minimization of such variability within focus groups often encourages discussion by increasing the likelihood of similarity in perceptions and experiences among participants. The maximization of such variability across focus groups often eases subsequent comparisons and data interpretation. Third, participants who are strangers to one another should be favored over acquaintances. Because acquaintances are more likely to share tacit, taken-for-granted assumptions, discussion among focus group members with stronger acquaintanceship ties can be relatively difficult to interpret, understand, and evaluate.

Group structure. As in the use of the conversational interview, the researcher must make decisions about the focus group's structure. A structured focus group has a preplanned set of agenda topics to be covered, a set of questions to be asked, and a particular desired level of moderator involvement. Typically, a structured format lends itself to discussion of issues that are relatively well understood or for which substantial theory already exists. In contrast, an unstructured focus group has a rather undefined and free-flowing nature. Such a group has only a general topic to guide discussion, questions are not commonly planned in advance, and the moderator strives to manage the group members' interactions as the immediate and changing conditions demand. Within a single focus group session, for example, the moderator may be very directive at times and relatively inactive at others. The unstructured format lends itself to discussion of issues that are poorly understood or for which minimal theory is available. Between the two extremes of structured and unstructured focus groups (and akin to the semistructured interview), a funnel format might be applied. In the beginning, the focus group might be relatively unstructured, but over time the moderator imposes increasing structure as he or she moves the group along a desired theme.

Group size and discussion quality. Decisions about a focus group's size will directly affect discussion quality. First, the quality of discussion depends heavily upon the participants' involvement with the topic: The greater their involvement, the more likely it is that an active and meaningful discussion will occur. In general, it is easier for members of smaller groups to have higher levels of involvement than it is for members of larger groups. In addition, the moderator should enter with a strong sense of the participants' likely involvement with the topic when the group is small. Second, discussion quality also depends upon the moderator's skill at managing individuals' participation. In a small focus group, for example, an individual's level of discussion can be inhibited by one or two other people. A talented moderator would quickly observe these inhibiting effects and intervene to stop them. In a large focus group, discussion quality can be lost if subgroups begin separate conversations. Again, a skilled moderator would quickly observe the signs that subgroups are forming and intervene to stop them. Thus, a moderator should enter with a realistic sense about his or her facilitation skills.

Number of groups. Although the number of focus groups that can be held is usually affected by cost considerations, ideally the researcher should allow theoretical saturation to determine the number of focus groups used. As noted in Chapter 3, theoretical saturation has been reached when holding one more focus group is not expected to lead to any new learning. More pragmatically, Morgan (1997) recommends that the researcher should conduct at least three focus groups on a given topic. With only a single focus group, the researcher cannot confidently discount the alternative explanation that results are due to the unique combination of participants. Even with the corroboration of a second focus group, confidence in the obtained results still remains somewhat weak. In Morgan's judgment, corroboration from a third group's results indicates that theoretical saturation may be near.

Criteria for evaluation. The criteria to be used to judge a focus group's success should be specified during the planning phase. Four "maximizing" standards for evaluating focus groups have been proposed (Merton, Fiske, & Kendall, 1990; Morgan, 1997). First, the *range* of topics covered during the focus group should be maximized. Operationally, for example, the number of topics, which were either preplanned or emergent, might be counted. Second, the *specificity* of these topics should be maximized. Operationally, for instance, participants' contributions to the discussion could be judged for their concrete and detailed nature. Third, the *depth* of these topics should be maximized. That is, the number of generalities (as opposed to concrete and detailed statements) made by focus group members could be counted as well. Fourth, *differences* in the personal contexts that individuals apply in the interpretation of these topics should be maximized. The number and nature of the personal contexts applied during the members' discussion might also be judged.

Miscellaneous issues. Two additional points merit brief comment. First, focus group members should not feel rushed. They should feel that enough time was scheduled for them to discuss the topic at hand fully. Depending upon the topic, available funding, and the researcher's prior experience, of course, the participants' expectations about the focus group's length might be set for 2 hours. The researcher should be aware that whereas he or she can always bring the session to an end before the allotted time is up if the discussion lags, it will probably not be possible to extend a session past the original expected length, because some (if not most) participants will likely have schedule conflicts. Second, topics should be organized similarly across focus groups. Such similarity can ease the management of group interactions and subsequent data analysis.

Conducting Focus Groups

Perhaps the most important determinant of a focus group's success is the moderator's level of skill in managing group interactions. This skill level is frequently related to the amount of prior experience a moderator has had. In particular, a good deal of prior experience often leads to a moderator's developing an individualized set of tacit knowledge and skills necessary for conducting successful focus groups. Newcomers to focus group research can best acquire needed moderator skills by observing and participating in focus groups. For experienced moderators, doing what has worked in the past may be the best and most specific advice possible.

Introductions. In a focus group, the members' sense of the discussion's flow, direction, and purpose is critical for success. It is imperative that, at the outset, the moderator set a tone conducive to subsequent discussion. The moderator might begin with candid statements about the overall topic for discussion and then relate his or her goals and expectations for the session. For example, the moderator might state that her intent is to learn what the members think about the topic at hand. By learning from several focus groups, she will not only better appreciate and understand the topic, but might become better positioned to inform others about the topic (e.g., educate managers, create theory). In addition, the moderator should offer general rules for the session; for example, only one person speaks at a time, everyone participates, and no one dominates discussion.

Beginning the discussion. A common tactic used by moderators to open focus group discussion is the icebreaker. For instance, the moderator might ask each participant in turn to tell the group his or her name and give some general biographical background (e.g., hometown, college degrees earned, marital status, names and ages of children) and specific information on his or her personal connection to the focus group's overall topic (e.g., given the topic, how and why are you participating). Sometimes, it may be appropriate to introduce humor; for instance, the moderator might ask each participant to relate the funniest experience he or she ever had at work. (It should be noted that many people are simply not humorous.) Through such preliminary interaction, participants usually become comfortable talking with one another. Ideally, following these opening exchanges, movement through a set of subsequent and preplanned questions occurs as a seamless transition.

Substantive discussion. As may be evident, there are no hard-and-fast rules for initiating, sustaining, and directing conversation. Issues of timing, sequencing, and probing follow from the unfolding circum-stances (as perceived by the moderator). Nonetheless, moderators often use the following three tactics to facilitate conversation. First, a modera-tor may reiterate participants' points or comments in order to help emphasize key issues that arise during discussion. This can effectively direct conversation toward a particular point or an entirely new topic. Second, a moderator may ask a participant for clarification of particular comments. This helps to freeze conversation on key points, immediately focusing attention and allowing for deeper discussion of those points. Third, a moderator may summarize participants' statements to help move the conversation along. This can serve to maintain (or enhance) the group members' sense of flow and direction.

Miscellaneous issues. Two additional issues should be noted. First, a focus group's physical site must balance the comfort of the participants and the demands on the researcher. For example, a convenient location for participants—such as at a nearby church, university, or community center—may be too expensive for the researcher to rent. Second, as noted above, focus group sessions are usually either audiotaped or videotaped. Often, audio recording is the method of choice because it can typically be accomplished unobtrusively. Microphones and other audio-recording devices easily blend into the background. In contrast, videotaping tends to be very obtrusive. More often than not, people talk and behave differently when they know they are being videotaped; it is difficult to be natural and spontaneous when a camera operator is moving around the room and sometimes pointing the camera directly at you.

Data Coding

There are three common techniques used for coding focus group data, and all three involve counting the number of times a key topic (or issue) is mentioned. The number of times a key topic is mentioned can be recorded according to (a) absolute frequency (the total number of times it is mentioned by any person), (b) frequency by individual persons (the average number of times the topic is mentioned by particular persons), and (c) frequency by individual focus group (the average number of times the topic is mentioned by a group). Moreover, the recorded fre-quencies might be compared with, for example, a prespecified conceptual structure (e.g., a theoretically derived taxonomy). Alternatively, these data may themselves be used to suggest a taxonomic structure.

Data Analysis

There are two tactics for data analysis. First, coding schemes are typically applied, and this often results in frequency counts. Methods of categorical data analysis might be applied (these are described in Chapter 6). Second, a portion of the focus group session might be devoted to the moderator's soliciting the participants' perceptions of what they have learned, or what others might learn, from the discussion. For example, indicators of a topic's importance can be (a) the number of groups that mentioned the topic, (b) the number of people within a group who mentioned the topic, and (c) verbal descriptions about how much energy and enthusiasm the topic generated. These data might be provided (i.e., fed back) to the participants during this designated period, and their interpretations elicited. Often, such interpretations can augment, confirm, or falsify the researcher's current understanding.

In addition, participants might be provided with some quantitative information, such as a rank ordering or rating of the importance of the various topics discussed. Although logistically complicated, a system could be set up whereby the various topics mentioned during the focus group's discussion could be counted as the discussion goes on, then immediately analyzed with categorical data methods (e.g., by a research team member using a laptop personal computer). These statistics could then be fed back to the participants, and their reactions recorded.

Case Study Research Techniques

Although case study methods may be used primarily to describe organizational phenomena, researchers often design their case research along theoretical propositions. Depending upon the specificity of these propositions, they can use their research to test or generate management theories. Thus, the techniques described below can be adapted to either purpose. In particular, pattern matching and time series methods are discussed. (Much of what follows is based on the work of Yin, 1994.)

Pattern Matching

Although I describe several variations below, all pattern matching involves two simple steps. First, an expected pattern among variables, events, acts, or some other phenomena of interest must be specified before case data are collected. Presumably, the expected pattern derives from a formal theory or set of (less formal) conceptual propositions. Second, the expected pattern is compared with subsequently collected empirical case data for its degree of fit. Note that the logic of pattern matching is no different from that applied to virtually any scientific endeavor. That is, ideas are subjected to empirical test.

Many theories involve multiple outcomes of interest (or dependent variables). Usually, a pattern of increases or decreases in these outcomes is predicted to correspond to changes in a set of theorized antecedent variables. In case study research, the investigator's task is to verify that the changes in antecedent and outcomes variables indeed occurred, but that these changes occurred under conditions set by the theory. Below, a running example is provided, with the job characteristics model as the tested theory. Variations of pattern matching are illustrated using this running example.

The job characteristics model. In their model, Hackman and Oldham (1980) theorize at least five sets of causal linkages. First, increases in a job's collective skill variety, task identity, and task significance enhance the meaningfulness of work. Second, increases in a job's autonomy enhance the experienced responsibility for the work's outcomes. Third, increases in a job's feedback enhance knowledge of the work's results. It should be noted that skill variety, task identity, task significance, autonomy, and feedback constitute the model's independent variables. Fourth, aggregate increases in the (a) meaningfulness of work, (b) responsibility for outcomes, and (c) knowledge of results *increase* an employee's job performance, job satisfaction, and organizational commitment but *decrease* the likelihood of the employee's turnover and absenteeism. Whereas meaningfulness, responsibility, and knowledge of results are the model's intervening variables, performance, satisfaction, commitment, turnover, and absenteeism constitute the model's dependent variables. Fifth, these linkages are stronger for employees with higher growth need strength and adequate levels of requisite job knowledge and skills. Thus, growth need strength and job knowledge and skills constitute the model's contextual (or moderator) variables.

Measurements. In case study research, each of the model's variables, linkages, and conditions might be measured as follows. First, analysis of engineering and purchase documents might verify whether *objective* changes to the company's computer system actually increased (or decreased) a job's levels of skill variety, task identity, task significance, autonomy, and knowledge of results. Second, employee interviews or participant observation could corroborate whether the theorized increases (or decreases) in employees' experienced meaningfulness, responsibility, and knowledge of results occurred. Third, analysis of individual personnel records or employee interviews could indicate whether job performance, job satisfaction, and organizational commitment increased and whether turnover and absenteeism decreased. Fourth, inspection of preemployment testing records might reveal individuals' levels of growth need strength and requisite knowledge, skills, and abilities.

Matching dependent variables. Presuming variables were validly measured and specified intervening and contextual conditions occur as theorized, pattern matching of the dependent variables involves judging whether these outcomes changed as theorized. For the job characteristics model, pattern matching of the dependent variable involves judging whether job performance, job satisfaction, and organizational commitment actually went up and whether turnover and absenteeism actually went down. If the predicted pattern is observed, corroboration of the model should be inferred. If the predicted pattern is not observed, falsification of the model should be inferred. If some portion of the expected pattern is observed, some corroboration or falsification can be inferred, depending upon one's preference of terms.

Matching independent variables. Pattern matching of the independent variables involves specification of one or more (if possible) mutually exclusive combinations of the independent variables and the subsequent observation of which combination of variables actually occurred. Under ideal circumstances, observation of one particular combination of dependent variables would preclude the others. For instance, the job characteristics model specifies that a *multiplicative combination* of skill variety, task identity, and task significance affects experienced responsibility. Subsequent observation that a linear, geometric, or otherwise noncompensatory combination of these components increases (or decreases) experienced meaningfulness constitutes falsification of this portion of the model. Similarly, subsequent observation that the specified multiplicative combination affected experienced responsibility or knowledge of results also constitutes falsification for this portion of the job characteristics model. (Autonomy is theorized to increase felt responsibility, and feedback is theorized to increase knowledge of results.)

Replication of matching dependent or independent variables. Although informative, single case studies must be viewed with caution. As in any study, replication is recommended. If a second organization holds an identical or a very similar set of a theory's variables and linkages as that found in the original case, a *literal* replication can be conducted. If, on the other hand, the second organization holds a different set of a theory's variables and linkages than that found in the first case, a more informative *theoretical* replication may be possible. Suppose, for example, the variables and linkages for the job characteristics model were validity measured in a second organization. Suppose further that the second organization's level of employee need growth strength was dramatically low, to the point of being virtual nonexistent. A theoretical prediction would be *no* (or minimal) change in the dependent variables. If a substantial change is observed in the dependent variables, theory falsification should be inferred, and replication did not occur. If no (or minimal) changed is judged to have occurred, theory corroboration should be inferred, and theoretical replication may have occurred. If a minimal change is judged, some corroboration or falsification can be inferred, and a partial replication might be inferred as well.

Time Series

Much like time series in quasi-experimental design (Cook & Campbell, 1979), time series can be conducted in case study research. A strength of case study research is that organizational phenomena and the local contexts in which they occur can be followed (prospectively) over time or reconstructed (retrospectively). One or more dynamic patterns for organizational events, acts, circumstances, or variables can be predicted; data can be collected (prospectively or retrospectively); and a comparison can be made between the predicted and empirical patterns. Alternatively, an expected pattern need not be predicted in advance. Instead, an empirical strategy could be followed, whereby the phenomena of interest are simply monitored or reconstructed.

Simple designs. With simple time series designs, the pattern of a minimal number of variables (e.g., one) and the contexts in which they occur are monitored over time. In the simplest design, a variable (e.g., employee's job performance) might be monitored over time in order to establish a base rate. On the one hand, observation of a slightly positive trend may be sufficient to inhibit managerial interventions, because such actions can be quite expensive or disruptive. On the other hand, a slightly negative trend may be sufficient to encourage managerial actions, because of concern for long-term consequences.

Slightly more complicated designs. In a slightly more complicated design, an *interrupted time series* might be applied. Sometimes, an intervention can be anticipated, such as the introduction of a new technology, compensation package, or organizational structure. If a base rate has been established during the preintervention period, changes in a monitored variable (e.g., job performance over time) before and after the intervention could be compared (judgmentally or statistically). Changes from the base rate after the intervention might be reasonably attributed to the intervention itself.

Still more complicated designs. In a still more complicated design, company or government records might allow for a historical reconstruction of a phenomenon's base rate across multiple operating units (e.g., output at a consulting firm's 10 branches located in different cities). Prospectively or retrospectively, the introduction of an intervention might be documented, and the levels of the phenomenon can be compared between pre- and postintervention periods across the multiple case replications. Changes from the base rate after the intervention might be reasonably attributed to the intervention itself. From these three simple variations, the strength of a causal inference is enhanced.

Complex designs. With more complex designs, changes in trends can be monitored or reconstructed over time. For example, the phenomenon of interest might be changes in output levels across three manufacturing plants after the introduction of team-based management. It might be expected, for example, that, in comparison to a base rate, output falls somewhat after the immediate implementation of teams because of ambiguities in the new system. After a year, it might be expected that output will increase substantially. With historical records of plant output, supplemented with interviews of people who worked in these three plants during the period under study, a predicted decrease followed by an increase in output could be compared with what actually happened. In addition to trend changes on a single variable, multiple variables could be monitored for single or multiple trends. For example, employee morale, turnover, and acts of sabotage may be of concern among those who survive three rounds of layoffs at 10 company plants. Because layoffs can often be anticipated well in advance, a prospective case design could be adopted. In particular, the three outcomes of interest could be monitored and base rates established. Based on various survivor theories (e.g., Noer, 1993), it might be predicted that survivors' morale and turnover would decrease and that acts of sabotage would increase. Immediately after each round of layoffs, the predicted pattern of the outcomes might be compared with their (a) base rate levels and (b) levels immediately after the prior layoff experience. Again, changes from the base rate after the intervention might be reasonably attributed to the intervention itself.

Chronologies. Like other forms of "more complex designs," chronological case studies also follow multiple variables and changes in trends over time. In addition, one or more of the following conditions are imposed onto data collection, analysis, interpretation, and display:

1. "Some events must always occur before other events, with the reverse *sequence* being impossible."
2. "Some events must always be followed by other events, on a *contingency* basis."

3. "Some events can only follow other events after a prespecified *passage of time.*"
4. "Certain *time periods* in a case study may be marked by classes of events that differ substantially from those of other time periods." (Yin, 1994, p. 117)

To the extent that one or more of these conditions can be met, it is often asserted that causal inferences are substantially strengthened.

Comment. Yin (1994) also delineates "lesser modes of analysis," for which he recommends survey data and other cross-case comparisons. In essence, Yin advocates "counting the countable" (Cassell & Symon, 1994). He cautions, however that such quantitative analyses may be difficult because of the inherently small sample sizes in case study research. Nonetheless, methods of categorical data analyses can and should be employed when feasible (e.g., Lee, Mitchell, Wise, & Fireman, 1996).

Conversational Interview Techniques

Planning the Conversation

A major characteristic of the conversational interview is its openness. To those who are unfamiliar with this methodology, a conversational interview may appear to be simply two individuals casually chatting about whatever comes to mind. In practice, the conversational interview is really much more than that. Although there are no hard-and-fast rules for the conduct of such interviews, researchers need to address several issues before they undertake to use this methodology. Below, I discuss the issues of thematizing, design, situation, criteria for evaluation (i.e., validity, which is also discussed in Chapter 6), and transcription as they relate to conversational interviews (see Table 4.2 for an overview of these issues). (Much of what follows is based on the work of Kvale, 1996.)

Thematizing. Because conversational interviews can be quite unstruc-tured (appearing aimless to some observers), the researcher should enter with a high degree of conceptual clarity as to the interrelationships

TABLE 4.2 Issues Involved in Conversational Interviews

Planning the conversational interview
  1. Thematizing the interview
  2. Designing the interview
  3. Focusing the situation
  4. The interview questions
  5. Judging the interview's quality

From speech to text
  1. Audiotaping
  2. Videotaping
  3. Field notes
  4. Working from memory

Transcriptions
  1. Reliability
  2. Validity

Major modes of data analysis
  1. Meaning condensation
  2. Meaning categorization
  3. Narrative structuring
  4. Hermeneutic meaning interpretation
  5. Ad hoc methods

Implications
  1. Triangulate with multiple modes of data analysis
  2. Create hybrid modes of data analysis

---

among the study's purpose, the research question, and the analytic method. In other words, the researcher should be able to articulate the conversational interview's themes as he or she begins the planning process. This thematizing, as it is sometimes called by qualitative researchers, might include reference to existing theory, literature, and the researcher's insight. Common themes include, for example, whether the conversational interview should be (a) exploratory or confirmatory, (b) relatively unstructured versus relatively structured, (c) intended to generate or test theory, and (d) the study's primary or secondary data collection method. To the extent possible, the researcher should do this thematizing in writing, and then share it with peers for informal review.

Comment. It might be noted that thematizing is sometimes too quickly overlooked by those qualitative researchers who hold a strong antipositivist orientation (e.g., some postmodernists). These researchers often want to begin directly with the design phase (discussed below). In particular, they frequently reject the value of prior and conceptual planning because it can be incompatible with a strong emphasis on reflexive research designs (i.e., sufficient flexibility to respond to local conditions). In other words, they prefer themes to emerge from the data and designs to be maximally contextualized (or highly sensitive to local conditions). Although certainly not wrong, these views may overly restrict the conversational interview technique to exploratory and theory-generating purposes. In my judgment, such limitations to the conversational interview minimize its practical value. Thus, I strongly encourage researchers to do as much thematizing (i.e., prior planning) as possible.

Design. Whereas *thematizing* refers to the articulation of what a study should do and why it should do so, *design* refers to the overall plan of how to conduct the study. It includes such technical issues as (a) the number of interviews to be conducted, (b) whether the interviews should include more factual versus more interpretative questions, and (c) whether the study's various parts lend themselves to (if not facilitate) the final outcome (e.g., a 40-page double-spaced journal submission). The acts of thematizing and design should clarify for the researcher in a compelling fashion when the conversational interview is well- versus ill-suited to the study in question. For example, Kvale (1996) suggests that conversational interviews should be avoided if thematizing or design reveals a researcher's interest to be in (a) estimating a population's parameter value, (b) the direct study of behavior, or (c) deeper understanding of organizational phenomena that operate at a tacit level.

Focusing the interview situation. The conversational interview involves two (or more) persons chatting on themes of mutual interest. However, the persons involved have an unequal power relationship. Almost always, the interviewer is the driving force. Thus, the interviewer's framing of the interview (how he or she defines the situation) for the interviewee becomes critical to success. Framing involves (a) explaining to the interviewee the interview's purpose (e.g., research study); (b) providing an overview of the interview agenda (i.e., topics and questions), the expected nature of responses, the extent of informality, and the probing nature of some follow-up questions; (c) stating that a debriefing will be provided at the interview's end; and (d) warning that field notes, tape recordings, or both will be made during the interview.

The interview questions. Kvale (1996, pp. 133-135) suggests that there are nine interrelated types of interview questions (listed below). Although these are presented in an apparent sequence, the informal and relatively unstructured nature of the conversational interview requires that the interviewer move back and forth among the various types of questions throughout the interview session, as the situation's dynamics suggest. Again, substantial interviewer skill, sensitivity, and insight are demanded.

1. *Introductory questions* elicit personal experiences about the phenomena understudy and frame subsequent questions. Typical introductory questions include the following: "Can you tell me about . . . ?"; "What happened when . . . ?"; and "Have you ever experienced . . . ?"

2. *Follow-up questions* serve, ideally, as seamless transitions to new issues. These questions should be asked in a sincere, curious, persistent, and critical manner, which can be enhanced by such interviewer behaviors as head nods, pauses, and prodding utterances (e.g., "yes"). In addition, the interviewer might notice and ask about the interviewee's unusual word choices, body language, and changes in intonation.

3. *Probing questions* are used to seek new information without necessarily stating the theme the interviewer wishes to pursue. Common probing questions include the following: "Could you say more about . . . ?"; "Can you give another example to help clarify . . . ?; and "What did you mean by . . . ?"

4. *Specifying questions* move the discussion toward greater specificity. These questions commonly follow more general questions or interviewee responses. For example, the interviewer might ask: "What did you actually do at that moment?"; "Did you have a physical, as well as emotional, reaction?"; and "Has this, or anything like this, ever happened before?"

5. *Direct questions* introduce new topics and themes. Because of their directness, they can be disruptive or jarring to the ongoing conversation. Interviewees can feel threatened and become inhibited during subsequent conversation. Thus, the interviewer must show considerable care and sensitivity in asking direct questions such as, "Have you ever stolen anything worth more than $10 dollars from work?" or "When dealing with your former boss, did you ever behave toward her in a mean-spirited fashion?" Given the potential sensitivity of direct questions, interviewees must feel that at least a modest degree of openness and trust has been established.

6. *Indirect questions* concern specific topics but allow for either specific or general responses. Interviewees may respond personally or in reference to a general group. For instance, "What are the typical reasons people quit their jobs here?" can be answered from the viewpoint of a general work group, a person who recently left, or the respondent's own likely behavior. Similarly, "What do you believe is the general morale around here?" can be interpreted and answered from multiple perspectives.

7. *Structured questions* are typically prewritten items that are used to shift conversation to a new topic when a current topic is unlikely to generate any more discussion. In approaching such a question, the interviewer might say, "I'd like to move to a new topic."

8. *Interpretative questions* involve restating, rephrasing, summarizing, or paraphrasing the interviewee's remarks. These questions often serve to facilitate conversation, redirect discussion, and avoid misunderstanding. The interviewer may begin, for example: "Let me see if I understand you—did you mean to say . . . ?"; "If I heard you correctly, you're saying . . . ?"; or "Let me summarize what you've said. . . ."

9. *Silence* is not technically a type of question, of course, but well-placed pauses (or "screaming gaps of silence"), augmented by the interviewer's expectant facial expressions, can often be quite effective at eliciting comments.

Interview quality. A high-quality conversational interview is one that earns affirmative answers to the following questions:

1. Was the conversation spontaneous, rich, and specific?
2. Were answers relevant to the questions asked?
3. Were the interviewer's questions short and the subject's responses long?
4. Did the interviewer follow up or clarify the meanings of the interviewee's answers throughout the interview?
5. Did the interviewer interpret interviewee responses throughout the interview?
6. Did the interviewer corroborate interpretations during the course of the interview?
7. Did the interview itself appear self-communicating?

High-quality work on the part of the interviewer is reflected by affirmative answers to the following questions:

1. Was the interviewer knowledgeable about the topic of the interview? That is, did he or she know what themes or aspects to pursue, and did he or

she determine that the interviewee had substantial background information about the organization and work context?

2. Did the interviewer impose sufficient structure on the interview? That is, did he or she make the experience appear neither too routinized nor too free-flowing?

3. Did the interviewer ask clear, understandable, and (usually) short questions? For instance, did the interviewee seldom need to ask for clarifications or restatements?

4. Was the interviewer sufficiently gentle or sensitive to the issue at hand? In other words, did he or she show empathy or tolerance for more ambiguous, less well articulated responses?

5. Was the interviewer a good listener? In particular, did he or she wait for the interviewee to complete responses, show interest in the responses, and respond quickly to new issues?

6. Was the interviewer critical? That is, because responses should not necessarily be taken at face value, did he or she conduct interpretation of the responses on an ongoing basis?

7. Was the interviewer able to remember and refer back to earlier discussion? That is, was he or she able to connect points and issues raised throughout the interview?

From Speech to Text

Conversational interviews are recorded most often through some combination of audio- or videotape, field notes, and simple memory; a combination of methods is useful because each of these recording methods has its strengths and weaknesses.

Audiotaping, videotaping, and field notes. Audiotape captures an exact record of the spoken conversation, but it does not record visual aspects of the physical context, facial expressions, or body language. Typically, however, the interviewer takes notice of these aspects of the interview and records such characteristics and their potential effects in extensive field notes. In contrast, videotape yields an exact record of the spoken conversation as well as much of the physical context and some of the nonverbal communication. However, the process of videotaping is quite obtrusive and can itself produce unintended effects. In comparison with "natural conversations," people often behave and verbalize differently while they are being videotaped. In addition, videotaping can produce a huge amount of data, attempted analysis of which may well overwhelm the researcher's personal and financial resources. Thus, the decision to videotape should be made with care. Whether the researcher decides to employ audio- or videotape, it is highly recommended that he or she also take extensive field notes to both supplement and enhance the interpretation of the mechanical tapes.

Comment. As we approach the new millennium, we often take product reliability for granted; however, mechanical failures still sometimes occur. Because conversational interviews are time-consuming for both parties and potentially difficult to reschedule, the interviewer must take steps to avoid mechanical failure. First, it is a good idea for the interviewer to bring along extra batteries, an extra tape recorder, or both. Second, the interviewer should not assume that he or she is familiar with the particular recording device to be used (e.g., how it might connect to a telephone). Further, the interviewer should be aware that such easily overlooked elements as poor placement of a microphone, a particular room's acoustics, and an interviewee's low, monotone voice can result in an inaudible recording.

Another comment. Although it is not advisable for an interviewer to try to rely on memory alone, on occasion this may become necessary. Once, my colleagues and I began a study with the strong general expectation that everyone we interviewed would be comfortable being audiotaped. We routinely asked for permission, but we never expected anyone to refuse it. We were quite startled and unprepared when one interviewee, who had volunteered to participate, requested no audiotaping or manual note taking. Although we wrote copious field notes immediately after the interview, the quality of those notes were suspect because of our lack of preparation. Eventually, we dropped the data from this interview from the study because of concerns over the data's reliability. Thus, as I have noted, although sole reliance on memory is ill-advised, my own experience suggests that a researcher should be prepared for the (fortunately few) situations when this may become necessary.

Transcripts

The recordings of conversational interviews are rarely analyzed directly. In addition to augmenting their field notes, researchers almost always have interviews transcribed. The reliability and validity of these transcriptions must be considered. Simply put, unreliable or invalid transcription renders a conversational interview useless.

Reliability. Ordinarily, a variation of interrater agreement is applied to estimate transcription reliability. For example, two persons type up separately an entire interview (or selected portions of an interview) using a computerized qualitative research software package. The program then identifies, locates in the file itself, and counts word differences between the two typed versions. (Many common word processing packages have this capability as well.) A percentage of correct overlap could be calculated as an estimate of reliability. An adequate, less dependable, but cheaper approach would be for one person to transcribe the text and another to compare the printed text with what he or she hears on the tape.

Comment. The estimation of reliability must be done. It is conceptually straightforward, mechanically simple, and compatible with the norms and values of the larger discipline of organizational science. More pragmatically, journal reviewers might (and should) require some meaningful estimate of reliability. A word of caution is in order, however. Because estimating transcript reliability can be so straightforward and mechanically simple, it is easy to underestimate the skills required of the typists. In a resource-rich environment, the use of professional transcribers can resolve many concerns. In a resource-poor environment, it is often convenient and cost-efficient to employ an undergraduate, master's, or doctoral student to do this work. I have used both professional and student transcribers in my own work, and I have found that whereas quality has been consistently high among the professionals, it has been extraordinarily variable across student transcribers. With respect to transcription, then, an old adage seems to apply: You get what you pay for.

Validity. In comparison to reliability, transcription validity is a far more difficult issue. Potentially, a transcription can fundamentally alter the original discourse's meaning. In no small way, the change from oral to written language often entails application of different rules. From the viewpoint of a strong adherent of postmodernism, for example, transcription directly decontextualizes and detemporalizes the text's meaning. To such a postmodernist, the text's meaning is thus so fundamentally altered that it is unlikely to be reflective of the actual interview. In other words, although reliable, the transcript is an invalid representation of the interview's content. To a more mainstream quantitative researcher, who may hold a more positivist view, a transcription does not necessarily alter a text's meaning in such a dramatic fashion. This latter researcher would likely perceive much more room for judging how much alteration has occurred. That is, there is room for an assessment of whether too much, insufficient, minimal, or no change in meaning has been made.

Comment. Because I discuss methods of estimating and judging validity in Chapter 7, further detail will be deferred. At this point, however, some researchers, particularly those who are very strong adherents of postmodernism, social construction, and emergent meanings, might pose the question of validity as, What is the correct transcription? Under those conditions and to those persons, the question may be impossible to answer. To the vast majority of "mainstream" qualitatively and quantitatively oriented management researchers, however, the question of validity might be posed differently. These persons might choose to ask, What is a useful transcription for research? In my judgment, the second question is more valuable than the first.

Major Modes of Data Analysis

I discuss below five modes of analyzing the interview data: meaning condensation, meaning categorization, narrative structuring, hermeneutic meaning interpretation, and ad hoc methods. It is important to note that each mode is typically individualized by different researchers. That is, each researcher tends to impose his or her own preferences and style in operationalizing the specific steps involved in each of these modes of data analysis.

Meaning Condensation

During meaning condensation, the researcher strives to extract, abridge, or abstract the most important themes from the data (i.e., the interview's text). As the name suggests, meaning condensation involves data reduction, while simultaneously articulating the data's most important themes. Meaning condensation can be seen as analogous (albeit somewhat loosely interpreted) to a statistical factor analysis, where the "latent roots" or underlying causal constructs from a correlation (or covariance) matrix are identified and extracted.

Meaning condensation typically involves five basic steps. First, one or more members of the research team read the entire transcript of an interview. (Some researchers prefer to complete the entire five-step analysis one interview at a time; others prefer to read across an entire set of interviews before beginning the second step. My personal preference is to do both—that is, I like to read across all interviews in order to develop a sense of the entire data set, and then analyze each conversational interview, one at a time.)

Second, the researcher identifies "natural meaning units," or portions of the text that are judged to relate to an identifiable theme (or issue). These natural meaning units can consist of sentence fragments, complete sentences, portions of paragraphs, or longer passages. The researcher pulls out these portions of text and reassembles them physically into a continuous flow of text. Before word processing packages made manipulation of portions of text easy, researchers would make photocopies of the text, cut out potentially connected portions, and array them on a tabletop or paste them onto other sheets of paper. The researchers would then make decisions as to these units' naturalness, holism, and relevance to an identifiable topic (or theme). Now, virtually any word processing package or software written for qualitative data analysis makes the gathering of potential natural units quite simple. Making decisions about their naturalness, holism, and relevance remains, however, a creative and challenging act of induction.

In the creation of natural meaning units, conceptual completeness, thoroughness of content, and substantive depth should be driving forces. Nonetheless, it is also advisable for the researcher to have some sense of how large a quantity of data is manageable. On the one hand, if too little text is extracted, the natural meaning unit may contain an insufficient amount of information and be uninterpretable. On the other hand, if too much text is extracted, the natural meaning unit may contain an overwhelming amount of information and also be uninterpretable. Returning to the earlier analogy to factor analysis, natural meaning units can be seen as akin to principle factors (or extracted latent traits).

Third, the natural meaning unit must be clearly defined. Sometimes this step is called thematizing because the unit's underlying theme (or latent trait) is to be conveyed. Often, a label and an accompanying short paragraph can effectively capture and convey the natural unit's substantive content. Like its creation, writing the natural meaning unit's definition is also a creative and challenging act. Unlike its creation, defining the unit is a deductive exercise.

Yin (1994) describes the fourth step as "interrogating the meaning units in terms of the specific purpose of the study" (p. 194). In other words, the researcher asks how each natural meaning unit fits with or informs the study's research questions. These meaning units are judged for how well they concisely capture and convey a major idea from the data.

Fifth, the concisely worded natural meaning units must be integrated into a coherent and nonredundant structure. That is, the larger data set must be reduced into a more meaningful, coherent, yet manageable set of underlying themes. Returning to the analogy to factor analysis, the outcome of meaning condensation is akin to the achievement of a factorial "simple structure."

Meaning Categorization

Whereas meaning condensation reduces the data to their most important themes, meaning categorization distributes statements from the interview data into quantifiable categories. These categories can be binary, such as "It occurs"/"It does not occur," or they can be ordinal, such as a rating of from 1 to 5 indicating an increasing magnitude for "it." The object of these categories (or the "it") can be a job attitude, work behavior, organizational characteristic, or other managerial phenomenon. The outcome of these categorizations can be analyzed qualitatively or quantitatively.

Meaning categorization usually involves four steps. First, the researcher must select an organizing conceptual structure that will serve as the basis for subsequent categorizing judgments. That is, the structure defines the phenomena and variables of interest. Moreover, it can be derived from an existing theory, model, or set of propositions from the literature, or it can be derived from the interview data themselves (in an iterative fashion with subsequent steps).

Second, the researcher must define as clearly as possible the focal attitudes, behaviors, organizational characteristics, and other phenomena of interest identified by the conceptual organizing structure. That is, the researcher must fully specify the characteristics or dimensions that will be evaluated subsequently. Ideally, these characteristics or dimensions are independent of one another. Less ideally, though certainly feasible, these characteristics (or dimensions) and their subdimensions might be modestly correlated (or dependent). The stronger this correlation, however, the more difficult will be the subsequent categorizations, analyses, and interpretations.

Third, one or (preferably) more evaluators must rate each interview transcription on each defined dimension. If, for example, there are 13 dimensions, each interviewee will have 13 scores. Presuming multiple evaluators, each dimension's binary or ordinal scores could be compared for interrater reliability.

Fourth, the researcher may analyze these scores qualitatively through the use of various graphic depictions (e.g., tables, charts, or cross-tabulations; see Miles & Huberman, 1994, for a compendium of display options). Alternatively, he or she may analyze the scores quantitatively, using categorical data analysis (described in Chapter 6) or more traditional methods (e.g., factor analysis, discriminant analysis, or regression).

Narrative Structuring

Whereas meaning condensation and meaning categorization seek to simplify data in a relatively straightforward manner, narrative structuring seeks to identify and reconstruct the interview text into longer stories. From responses to open-ended questions (e.g., Can you tell me, please, about the situation and circumstances surrounding the last time you quit your job?) or across several sequential questions (e.g., [a] Was there a particular event that first caused you to think about leaving? [b] Was that event expected or unexpected, positive or negative, or work or nonwork related? [c] Did that event lead directly to quitting or did that event lead to a careful comparison of the pluses and minuses of quitting?), a continuing narrative can sometimes be detected. Through the extraction and rearrangement of relevant text, a more continuous, coherent, integrative, and engaging single story can be recovered. Such a recovered narrative can often stimulate insight into the explanations for an organizational phenomenon of interest.

The work of narrative restructuring involves three steps. First, the researcher reads the transcribed interview as a whole. Second, he or she undertakes subsequent readings to identify temporal sequences, recurring social dimensions, and any overall plot in the text. Third, the researcher goes through an interactive (i.e., trial-and-error) process of physically arranging and rearranging the text itself, using a conventional word processing package or qualitative data analysis software.

Ultimately, the ideal outcome would be one or more compelling narrations. Each narration should be complete, with a beginning, a story or plot, and an ending, and each narration would be presented as a "stand-alone" story.

Hermeneutic Meaning Interpretation

In meaning condensation, meaning categorization, and narrative structuring, the researcher's interpretation is drawn almost exclusively from the interview text itself. In contrast, hermeneutic meaning interpretation requires that the researcher *impose* meaning based on the perspectives from a preexisting paradigm. For example, interview texts might be interpreted from such well-known perspectives as psychoanalysis, literary criticism, feminism, or the philosophy of Karl Marx or Ayn Rand. Because the mechanics of hermeneutic meaning interpretation vary according to the requirements of the adopted paradigm, specific steps and outcomes cannot be readily prescribed in advance. However, it is quite common for such interpretations to vary greatly in length; some may be longer than the original interview transcriptions themselves (e.g., a literary critique of a poem).

Ad Hoc Methods

In the four modes described above, the logic and mechanical steps involved in data analysis can be more or less anticipated. As the name suggests, ad hoc methods involve the application of any technique, based on either personal preference or trial and error. Miles and Huberman (1994, pp. 245-246), for example, describe 13 tactics that can be useful in the ad hoc interpretation of texts. Going from primarily descriptive to explanatory (Kvale, 1996), these tactics are as follows:

1. Noting patterns and themes
2. Seeing plausibility
3. Clustering
4. Applying metaphors
5. Counting
6. Comparing and contrasting
7. Partitioning variables
8. Subsuming particulars under general categories
9. Factoring
10. Noting relations between variables
11. Finding intervening variables
12. Building a logical chain of evidence
13. Creating theoretical coherence (i.e., theory building)

Conclusion

Although the techniques described in this chapter are associated with focus groups, case study research, and conversational interviews, it should not be overlooked that application of *multiple* techniques is highly advised. In other words, no method is perfect, and it is only prudent to triangulate with multiple methods. In addition to the techniques described here, the methods described in Chapter 5 (and the quantitative methods described in Chapter 6 as well) can often be quite appropriate for use in organizational research. Thus, researchers may want to design some of the techniques described in Chapters 5 and 6 into their studies (e.g., in two-phase or mixed-methodology designs).

5

Generic Techniques for Qualitative Research

Like Chapter 4, this chapter adopts a "how-to" orientation to describe generic techniques for qualitative research. However, the techniques discussed here are not necessarily associated with specific qualitative methods. Insofar as space constraints allow, this chapter presents a compendium of general approaches and specific techniques. In particular, participation and observation, interviewing, document construction and analysis, and the presentation of audiovisual data are discussed. A nontraditional example on job analysis is provided. Overall, the description in this chapter moves from the more general to the more specific.

Overview of Generic Techniques

In a panoramic sweep, the major techniques used in qualitative research are (a) participation and observation, (b) interviewing, (c) document construction and analysis, and (d) presentation of audiovisual data (Creswell, 1994; Marshall & Rossman, 1995). These techniques and their specific operationalizations are discussed in this chapter. Most organizational researchers are likely familiar with participation and observation techniques, but the use of interviews, document construction and analysis, and audiovisual data merits brief introductory comment. Chapters 3 and 4 have provided substantial coverage of conversational interviews and focus groups (or group interviews); in this chapter, I discuss addi-

TABLE 5.1   Issues Involved in the Use of Generic Qualitative
Research Techniques

Major types of techniques
  1. Participation and observation
  2. Interviewing
  3. Document construction and analysis
  4. Presentation of audiovisual data

Generic steps in qualitative data analysis
  1. Sorting
  2. Organizing
  3. Indexing

Major goals for qualitative data analysis
  1. Decomposition and reduction
  2. Reconstruction and expansion

Implications
  1. Does theory *guide* what the researcher looks for?
  2. Does theory *result from* what the researcher sees?

---

tional interview techniques that researchers can use to probe for more detailed and targeted information. The technique of document construction and analysis includes archival searches of, for example, official and unofficial company documents, journals or logs (often found in museums), and personal letters or diaries from individuals' private files. In addition, it can include the construction of such documents through narratives and life histories. In contrast to document construction and analysis, which typically involves some form of verbal text (e.g., memos or oral stories), audiovisual data presentation usually involves nontext sources, such as photographs, compact disks, software, and physical sites (e.g., studying a physical work location during off-hours, when the workers are gone). Metaphorically, one might think of document construction and analysis and the presentation of audiovisual data as akin to the anthropologist's or historian's work in a distant field site. Table 5.1 summarizes the issues involved in the use of generic qualitative research techniques.

Generic Analyses in Qualitative Techniques

The main techniques for analyzing qualitative data involve various applications of sorting, organizing, and indexing data (Mason, 1996).

Maxwell (1996), for example, recommends that this data sorting, organizing, and indexing (or coding) take place through the use of theoretical memos (see Chapter 3). Through a series of theoretical memos, the data are examined, categorized, reexamined, and recategorized into increasingly homogeneous groups. At each iterative step, the theoretical memos record the researchers' statements that directly compare and contrast these theorized categories. Over numerous passes at comparing and contrasting, a coherent conceptual structure should emerge.

In addition to categorization based on similarity, Maxwell (1996) also recommends that the data should be simultaneously contextualized. *Contextualizing* refers to the researcher's identification and articulation of distinct conceptual linkages between the emergent categories and their surrounding context. Thus, at each stage of memo writing, the researcher also produces contextualizing statements (or arguments) that connect the emerging homogeneous groups to their contexts. When taken together, parsimonious structures should be achieved through categorizations based on the *similarity* within groups and the specification of these groups' *dependence* on the surrounding context.

Although it can appear so, the process of data sorting, organizing, and indexing does not take place in a series of mechanical steps. Rather, it should be a creative act. Coffey and Atkinson (1996), for instance, describe two typical modes for creative data analysis. First, qualitative researchers can *decompose* and *reduce* their data. That is, the data are organized such that a general, coherent, and (above all) simplifying structure is imposed. The imposed structure of categories (or codes) must serve to facilitate the researcher's retrieval and manipulation of data. As suggested in Chapter 4, this process is analogous to a statistical factor analysis, where the data's underlying latent roots are identified.

Second, qualitative researchers can *reconstruct* and *expand* their data. Rather than simplifying, this effort purposefully transforms, reconceptualizes, and therefore complicates the data. Heuristic devices are most often applied. For example, would the already and subsequently to be collected data fit within an "input → throughput → output" logic? Can the data be classified into an "antecedents and consequences" framework? Can the data be categorized into a standard taxonomy of "job knowledge, skills, abilities, and performances" (or KSAPs)? By applying such heuristic devices, researchers should evoke new and broadening perspectives from the data.

At some point, and regardless of the specific analytic technique, qualitative researchers must move from data coding to interpretation. Thus, it is critical that researchers decide what role theory should play during their planning (or thematizing; see Chapter 3) phase. In particular, should an existing theory or conceptual structure *guide* what the researcher looks for in the data and how those data might be configured? Moreover, the application of existing theory implies its testing rather than its creation. (From an alternative view, some qualitative researchers might argue that theory overly restricts, rather than simply guides, what one looks for or at in the data.) Alternatively, should a theory or conceptual structure constitute the researcher's *end product*, which suggests theory creation rather than theory testing? Below, the major techniques (i.e., participation and observation, interviewing, document construction and analysis, and presentation of audiovisual data) and some of their corresponding analytic strategies are discussed.

Participation and Observation

Most often, participation and observation studies are assumed best suited to the study of phenomena that (a) involve interpersonal interactions and interpretations, (b) are controversial, (c) are hidden from public view, and (d) are not well understood (Waddington, 1994). Although most commonly applied to theory creation, participation and observation studies can effectively test theory as well. Whereas the data can certainly lead to the induction of research propositions, preexisting theory can also guide (or restrict) what the researcher looks for and how he or she configures the observed data.

Qualitative researchers commonly distinguish four classes of participant observers (Burgess, 1984; Creswell, 1994; Waddington, 1994):

1. *The complete participant:* This researcher participates fully but covertly as an organizational member. In addition, the researcher takes precautions to hide his or her scientific intentions, role, and observational activities. The researcher establishes and nurtures normal work and personal relationships with other organizational members.
2. *The participant as observer:* This researcher participates fully but overtly as a researcher; his or her scientific intentions, role, and observational activi-

ties are public and not hidden. The researcher establishes and nurtures normal work and personal relationships with other organizational members.

3. *The observer as participant:* This researcher participates as if he or she were an organizational member, and makes no effort to hide his or her scientific intentions, role, and observational activities. Although friendship ties can (and often do) form, the researcher is relatively passive in establishing and nurturing ties with organizational members.

4. *The complete observer:* This researcher remains in the background and watches and listens to (a) what others do, (b) what they say, and (c) the circumstances in which these actions and comments occur. As much as possible, the researcher remains unobtrusive; he or she is unlikely to form friendship ties with organizational members.

The primary advantages of participation and observation studies derive from the firsthand knowledge gained about organizational phenomena as they occur (a) in a real-world context, (b) in real time, and (c) without the prompting of potential distortions (or discomfort) from post hoc verbal descriptions. Such firsthand knowledge tends to be rich in contextualized detail, vivid to the observer, but minimized in academic research reports.

The primary disadvantages of participant observation studies stem from the potential for conflict between researchers' efforts to establish trust and their possible observation of unethical situations and acts. Waddington (1994), for example, describes the conflict he experienced when, after having spent considerable time and effort establishing trust among union members, he learned about possible plans for illegal, physically dangerous, and potentially life-threatening acts of violence related to union strike activities. The issues Waddington faced included whether or not he should inform the police and whether or not he should violate the trust placed in him by the union members. Further, not inconsequential to his career was the likelihood that his informing the police and losing the trust he had established among the union members would all but guarantee the unsuccessful end of his dissertation research.

Varying according to the level of (a) participation versus observation, (b) specific field constraints, and (c) financial and personal resources, of course, data from virtually all participation and observation studies will eventually be manifested as some form of field notes. Routinely, researchers conducting participation and observation studies will record extensive field notes daily (or as frequently as the situation allows).

These field notes may be (a) written as theoretical memos (see Chapter 3), which could be analyzed concurrently or later in time; (b) written as pure descriptions, which could be deposed and reduced or reconstructed and expanded later in time (Coffey & Atkinson, 1996); or (c) analyzed from a grounded theory orientation (see Chapter 3). In addition, the five major modes of analysis used for conversational interview data can be readily applied to participant observational studies. That is, the text of field notes may be subjected to meaning condensation, meaning categorization, narrative structuring, meaning interpretation, or ad hoc methods (see Chapter 4).

Comment

Participant observation techniques are very much underutilized in management research, though some well-known and exemplary studies exist (e.g., Adler & Adler, 1988; Sutton & Rafaeli, 1988; Van Maanen, 1975). The potential of these techniques to produce substantial insight through the generation or testing of theory, and more rigorously than one might expect, is too often overlooked.

Two observations seem particularly relevant to organizational researchers. First, any researcher, organizational or otherwise, surely appreciates the labor-intensiveness and necessity for longitudinal designs in participant observer studies. On the one hand, most assistant professors, who have a standard 5- or 6-year pretenure period, may well know and have been wisely advised to think very carefully about the career implications before engaging in participant observation studies. On the other hand, doctoral students typically have a window of a year or more in which to conduct their dissertation research. Although participant observation studies may not be advisable for assistant professors, doctoral students—presuming the overt support of their dissertation committees—might be well positioned in their programs and their careers to consider conducting such research.

Second, some of the best participant observation studies have been conducted by anthropologists and sociologists. Yet few of these successful researchers have done more than one—and very rarely more than two—such study. That is, these researchers seldom return to the field. Presumably, the mental, physical, and financial demands of participant observation studies discourage most people from returning to the field.

In my opinion, it takes an extraordinarily dedicated individual to conduct one participant observation study, let alone two. In addition to their structural positions in their programs and careers, however, dissertating doctoral students may also be well suited, in terms of social, physical, emotional, and financial well-being, to the demands of participant observation studies.

Taken together, the above observations lead me to strongly encourage faculty committees in management departments to support and nurture student ambitions to conduct participant observation studies. Both the students and, equally important, the management discipline will surely benefit.

Interviewing

Focus groups and conversational interviews, discussed in Chapter 4, represent relatively broad, general interviewing methods. In this section, I describe more focused, narrower techniques. Although these techniques are well suited to interview studies, it is important to note that they can be used in a variety of research designs, such as more traditional surveys or experiments. Below, I discuss the 20 statements test (Rees & Nicholson, 1994; Spitzer, Couch, & Stratton, 1973), question asking (Johnson & Briggs, 1994), protocol analysis, and repertory grids. Table 5.2 provides a summary of these interview techniques.

The 20 Statements Test

The 20 statements test originates from the social interactionist perspective, which places the "self" as the focal agent for interpreting the social world (Mead, 1934). This technique provides data on how individuals make sense of their world. Interviewees (or questionnaire respondents) are asked to give 20 answers to the question, Who am I? Through their responses (or statements), individuals are assumed to be interpretatively positioning themselves in the world. By structuring these statements, a researcher can readily depict the respondents' interpretations and worldviews, depending upon whether the researcher takes the data literally, interpretatively, or reflexively (see Chapter 3).

TABLE 5.2 Specific Interview Techniques

Technique	Purpose
20 statements test	Identifies and details individual's social (or organizational) world and specific place in that world
Question asking	Identifies and details individual's moment-by-moment decision-making processes during a preselected task
Protocol analysis	Identifies and details individual's moment-by-moment decision-making processes, with emphasis on cognitive processes, personal reasoning, and unique interpretations
Repertory grid	Depicts the personal constructs the individual uses to make sense of (or interpret) his or her social (or organizational) world

The specific categorization system used for responses to the 20 statements test depends upon the study's particular research questions and theoretical grounding (i.e., whether it is generating or testing theory). However, a common taxonomy is to classify statements into one of the following four groups (Rees & Nicholson, 1994):

- *Group A:* Self-conceptions about current physical characteristics (e.g., I have the physical features typical of Han Chinese).
- *Group B:* Self-identity based on social roles and structures (e.g., I am a business professor).
- *Group C:* Self-concept based on social roles and structures (e.g., I have little fear of failure), which is labeled *reflective self.*
- *Group D:* Other self-abstractions that do not fit into the three prior groups (e.g., I am a mammal), which are labeled *oceanic.*

Depending upon the researcher's interview and research questions, these categories may be insufficiently detailed, and additional categorizing statements may be required. As needed, then, additional categories or subcategories can be created. In a study described by Rees and Nicholson (1994), for example, the above category for Group C was deemed insufficient, because it included too many statements. As a result, the following subcategories were added:

1. Ideological beliefs (e.g., one's intuition about the overall scheme of the world, and how one fits into that schema)
2. Interests in the objects in one's social world

3. Personal ambition (e.g., expectations about status, role, or accomplishments)
4. Self-evaluations (e.g., images about how "important others" perceive one)

Through such categorizations, a conceptual structure can be gleaned from the data that depicts how interviewees interpret their social (or organizational) world, and conceptual propositions can then be derived. Alternatively, preexisting theory can identify categories a priori, and researchers can identify statements that fit these predetermined theory-based categories. Two or more researchers can independently classify the set of statements to estimate interrater reliability. For example, an empirical estimate of reliability can be the percentage of agreement between these raters.

Question Asking

Question asking is a method used to collect data on people's moment-by-moment decisions; it has been used frequently in the study of expert and computer systems (Briggs, 1990). As part of an interview (or experiment), a person is typically assigned a task to perform, and the questions the individual asks while performing the assigned task form the data that are recorded and analyzed.

Johnson and Briggs (1994) describe five steps for conducting question asking. First, the researcher should specify the level and range of (job) knowledge, skills, abilities, and performance that are of interest prior to any application of question asking. For example, should the interviewees (or the experiment's participants) be new hires, who would have minimal organizational experience but constitute a key determinant of future corporate effectiveness? Should the interviewees be recent retirees, who have substantial organizational experience but do not constitute a likely determinant of future firm success? Alternatively, what mix of new, experienced, and former employees might be selected to maximize variability on experience or future corporate effectiveness?

Second, the researcher must select a task for assignment. The task should have a clear beginning and ending. On the one hand, the task should not be completely foreign to the interviewee, because too much task ambiguity can preclude sufficiently formed or articulated questions.

On the other hand, the task should not be completely familiar, because too much task knowledge can preclude the necessity to ask any questions.

Third, the interviewees perform the assigned task. During the initial explanation phase, the interviewer describes the task's start and end points, provides information about procedures and any required equipment, and solicits questions (which are presumed to be the beginning of the moment-by-moment decision-making process). While the interviewee performs the task, the interviewer encourages all ongoing questions, which are presumed to reflect directly the subject's moment-by-moment decision-making process.

Fourth, data are recorded. Depending upon the study's research question and resource constraints, the data might be audio- or video-taped. On the higher side of technology, computers have recorded task performance (e.g., Briggs, 1990). On the lower side of technology, manual recording, using secretarial shorthand methods, might be applied (e.g., Briggs, 1988).

Fifth, the observed data are analyzed. In a grounded theory approach, for example, the generated questions might be analyzed through the use of theoretical memos (see Chapters 2 and 3). Alternatively, the five major modes for analyzing text-based data from conversational interviews might be applied (i.e., meaning condensation, meaning categorization, narrative structuring, meaning interpretation, and ad hoc methods; see Chapter 4).

Protocol Analysis

Protocol analysis also provides data on moment-by-moment decisions, but it offers a more focused depiction of the individual's decision-making processes, reasoning, and interpretations (Ericsson & Simon, 1984). More specifically, protocol analysis asks interviewees about "what they are doing, why they are doing it, what they are about to do, what they hope to achieve . . . with respect to a particular task or behaviour" (Johnson & Briggs, 1994, p. 61). Like question asking, protocol analysis is commonly used in the study of human-computer interactions. In contrast to asking questions during task performance (which are then recorded by the researcher), the participant in protocol analysis "talks through," "thinks aloud," or "concurrently verbalizes" *while* he or she performs an assigned task.

Johnson and Briggs (1994) describe the five steps taken in the conduct of protocol analysis. First, the researcher must judge whether the organizational context, situation, or domain allows for effective protocol analysis. In particular, the researcher must decide whether any of the following preclude, inhibit, or facilitate participants' abilities to provide the required "running commentary": (a) specific characteristics of the job task and surrounding organization (e.g., the task's naturally occurring cycle from beginning to end may be too brief to allow verbalizations), (b) participants' cognitive abilities (e.g., their verbal skills may be insufficient for them to describe complex tasks), and (c) feasibility of recording the verbalizations (e.g., recording devices themselves can inhibit or fundamentally alter some persons' speech).

Second, the researcher must assemble the task's materials and be sure that the participants are sufficiently practiced at verbalizing. Instructions for carrying out the task should have been written down and pilot tested previously for understandability. Tools and equipment should be in good working order. Perhaps most important, the participants should be practiced at *describing* their thought processes. It can be quite easy or tempting for a participant to verbalize what he or she thinks the researcher wants to hear (e.g., socially desirable responses).

Third, the verbalized protocols (or running commentaries) are recorded, usually on audio- or videotape. (Recall the discussion about the potential problems with recording devices in Chapter 4, however.)

Fourth, any taping is augmented by visual observation of task behaviors and field notes. That is, the researcher assigns someone to be responsible for watching, listening, and subsequently describing whatever transpires. A comparison between the recordings and the observer's notes can be taken as an indicator of reliability and possibly validity.

Fifth, the verbalized (and transcribed) data are analyzed. The transcribed text may be analyzed using the methods described in Chapters 3 and 4 (e.g., meaning condensation, meaning categorization, narrative structuring, meaning interpretation, and ad hoc methods). Estimates of reliability can readily follow.

Repertory Grids

Repertory grids depict how individuals make sense of (or interpret) their social or organizational world. Conceptually, the method derives from personal construct theory (Kelly, 1955). It has been used both to supplement interviews and as a stand-alone technique (Gammack & Stephens, 1994). Repertory grids fit within the philosophical traditions of constructivism, which holds the following:

1. "All communications and all understanding are a matter of interpretive construction on the part of the experiencing subject."
2. "The world . . . makes no claim whatsoever about 'truth' in the sense of correspondence with an ontological reality."
3. "Structures are viable [and] reality limits what is possible." (Glaserfeld, 1984, p. 24)

Furthermore, Gammack and Stephens (1994) add the following clarifications to the constructivist tradition:

1. "Humans attribute meaning, it is not a simple property of the referent."
2. "Meaning is negotiated through social action and dialog."
3. "Socially recognized knowledge constructions are adapted through interaction in a linguistic fashion." (p. 74)

When the above six points are considered together, the ideas that underlie repertory grids suggest that an interviewee holds some constructed sense of his or her place within the organization's social world. The interviewer's task, then, is to *probe* for the interviewee's existing mental structures (i.e., his or her cognitive maps) or to *negotiate* with the interviewee for the construction of that cognitive map. In both cases, the interviewer's role can be quite proactive.

According to Kelly (1955), the outcome of a repertory grid is a personal system of constructs that are stated in the interviewee's own terms and categories. Moreover, these constructs can be preexisting or developed during the interview.

The construction of a repertory grid involves three steps. First, the interviewer elicits potential construct elements. He or she might begin, for example, by asking the following general questions:

1. Could you please describe for me your typical day at work?
2. What constitutes particularly good (or bad) job performance?
3. What are your main responsibilities?

4. Who benefits (or suffers) from your doing a particularly good (or bad) job?
5. Who do you regularly come into contact with at work?

From the interviewee's responses, the interviewer seeks to identify specific elements. For instance, a high-voltage maintenance electrician might respond to the first question above with specific references to (a) arriving at an electrical substation to receive the day's assignment, (b) receiving the expected assignment, (c) planning for the assigned task, (d) assembling the necessary tools and equipment for easy access, (e) driving to the assigned work site, (f) conducting the behaviors required to perform the assigned maintenance task, and (g) documenting the completed work. From these statements, the interviewer might infer the following as elements of the interviewee's mental mapping of her or his work world: (a) punctuality; (b) listening and asking questions; (c) mentally practicing and anticipating the task's performance and accomplishment; (d) physically gathering the anticipated tools and equipment needed for task completion; (e) driving a truck; (f) highly specific task knowledge, skills, and abilities; and (g) knowledge of documentation procedures.

Second, the interviewer proposes and tests potential constructs that unify the elicited elements with subsequent questioning. The interviewer might suggest to the interviewee, for example, that the seven elements listed above might be simplified into (or subsumed by) a single construct labeled *task accomplishment*. Furthermore, the interviewer might ask additional probing questions to disconfirm or corroborate whether one or more of the elicited task elements actually fit within the proposed construct label. By repeating this process with additional questions, the interviewer can elicit more elements and propose more potential unifying constructs. With more probing questions, the interviewer can also test whether particular elements fit better within one or another of the constructs.

Third, the sets of tentative constructs and their elements are depicted as a repertory grid. In one of several possible repertory grids, Gammack and Stephens (1994) describe the following. The (simplifying) personal constructs are arrayed as the grid's "i-columns." The elements are arrayed as the grid's "j-rows." Correspondingly, there would be ij cells (i.e., the number of cells equals i times j) constituting the repertory grid (or depicted matrix). Within each of the grid's cells, the interviewer or the interviewee can assign a numeric value that represents the element's importance to the corresponding construct. For instance, the researcher might adopt a 5-point Likert scale, anchored from 1, *very unimportant*, to 5, *very important*. Within each interviewee's repertory grid or across the set of interviewees' grids, these assigned numeric values could be quantitatively analyzed (see Chapter 6).

Document Construction and Analysis

Typically, document analysis and construction involves the study of public and private documents, such as minutes of meetings, newspapers, and personal journals, diaries, and letters. The strengths of this method include the opportunity it gives the researcher to examine texts written in the participant's own words, and often with substantial care, its unobtrusiveness, and the need for relatively little transcription. Its weaknesses include potential difficulty in obtaining access to documents, the physical and financial costs that may be involved in the researcher's traveling to the documents, incompleteness of some texts, and difficulty in authenticating documents (Creswell, 1994, p. 151).

To date, document construction and analysis has not been broadly applied by organizational researchers, thus I will discuss this technique only briefly. The strengths of this method suggest that its potential usefulness may grow as the academic study of management addresses new, dynamic, and controversial social issues. Document construction and analysis may become a valued tool of organizational researchers in the future. In this section, I first present the basic technique of document analysis, the "hermeneutic interpretation of company documents" (Forster, 1994). Then, I discuss tracer studies (Hornby & Symon, 1994), which constitute a more specialized technique. Finally, I present quite briefly the use of narratives and life histories. Table 5.3 summarizes the specific techniques used in document construction and analysis.

Hermeneutic Interpretation of Company Documents

The hermeneutic tradition involves the study of texts. It assumes that all text-based meaning is negotiated, and texts, therefore, involve self-

TABLE 5.3 Specific Techniques Used in Document Construction and Analysis

Technique	Purpose
Hermeneutic interpretation of company documents	A deeper understanding of text of materials
Tracer studies	Insight into organizational processes gained from following a preselected "tag" through formal or informal systems
Narratives and life histories	Personal explanations (or stories) of individuals' lives, specific experiences, or how well individuals fit into an organization's social system

presentation, secrecy, hidden agendas, and political manipulations. As a result, hermeneutic researchers must delve into deeper meanings. Indeed, Forster (1994) notes: "The interpretation of these texts is governed by a hermeneutic spiral. The understanding of disparate (and often contradictory) texts evolves upward through a spiral of understanding" (p. 150).

This hermeneutic spiral involves six generic steps to the study of company documents. First, the researcher extensively and intensively reads and rereads the text materials in order to move beyond a superficial understanding. Through such efforts, the texts' underlying themes and tacit, taken-for-granted assumptions should become evident. Second, the researcher clearly articulates the texts' identified themes. Most often, these themes will appear to diverge and to be contradictory. Third, the researcher thematizes the data by clustering or imposing order onto these themes. Simultaneously, this coherent packaging, structuring, or thematizing must meaningfully reduce the data. In Chapter 4, I made an analogy between such thematizing and statistical factor analysis; that analogy holds here as well.

As noted, the first three steps involve the researcher's understanding the texts while simultaneously striving to reduce them. The fourth step begins the analysis. The researcher compares the thematized (or meaningfully reduced and therefore more coherent) data with other texts. By *triangulating* the constructed interpretations across multiple sources of additional and independent texts, the researcher can corroborate or falsify the imposed categories (or simplifying structure). In the fifth step, the researcher employs as many reliability and validity checks as possible. Using the results of the triangulation and the reliability and validity

checks, the researcher can then modify the thematized data. In herme-
neutical terms, the data are recontextualized. In the sixth step, the
researcher finalizes the data in an academic research document or applied case report.

Tracer Studies

A tracer study provides data on organizational processes by following
how a "tag" moves through a social system. By way of physical analo-
gies, for example, tracer studies have been used to study water currents
in an ecosystem by monitoring how colored dye moves through a
subsystem of rivers and streams (Mossman, Holly, & Schnoor, 1991) and
to study blood flows in a human circulatory system by monitoring how
opaque fluids move through the subsystem of veins, arteries, and organs
(Walsh, 1978). In both these examples, the tags were observable foreign
substances introduced by researchers. In an organizational context,
Hornby and Symon (1994) studied how potential weaknesses evolved
as a government agency computerized its clerical support system. Their
tag was the agency's formal "Change Request Document," which recorded the participants' recommended changes as a new computerized
clerical support system was implemented. Through these formal documents (i.e., tracer tags), points of ineffectiveness could be identified, and
individuals who offered suggested changes could be interviewed for
richer detail.

As applied in organizational contexts, tracer studies involve five basic
decisions. First, the researcher must identify and select one or more
potential tags. A tag can be any recorded (or at least recordable) entity in
a system. As in the examples above, tags can be found in human, product,
machine, or accounting processes. Moreover, tags are often manifested
in overt decisions, observable actions, official minutes of meetings, and
official or unofficial company records. In selecting tags, a researcher
might show bias toward preexisting theoretical criteria and structures.
The more developed this theory, and the more clearly it is understood
by management researchers, the easier, clearer, and more interpretable
are the tags' subsequent application. A researcher might also show bias
toward tags that represent well-accepted and well-understood individual or organizational variables (e.g., job performance, return on equity,

number of errors). In both cases, attention moves more quickly from what the tags indicate to what the researcher learns from following the tags.

Second, the researcher must determine the points in the organizational process at which data are to be collected. Hornby and Symon (1994) label these the "sampling criteria" (p. 173). In some cases, it may be possible to monitor a tag through an entire process. For example, a defective product (i.e., the tag) might be introduced into a manufacturing facility's quality control system and then followed until the defect is detected or corrected. In other circumstances, it may be possible to monitor a tag only during preselected points in a process. For instance, hypothetical résumés might be created for several particularly strong and weak job candidates and entered into a firm's college recruitment system. Through the monitoring of predetermined well-defined points in the hiring system (e.g., sequential evaluations by the campus representative, her immediate recruitment supervisor, and their departmental manager), inconsistencies in the decision-making process might be detected (and subsequently resolved).

Third, the researcher must judge the selected (or constructed) tag for its contextualization. Although the tag may fit within one particular system, it may not fit well with other coexisting or larger organizational systems. In other words, the researcher must judge the tag's compatibility with multiple organizational processes. Take the above example of the sequential evaluations of hypothetical job candidates (i.e., the tags) by human resource persons. In such a case, although consistency of the recruiting system may be readily assessed, the persons making the decisions may feel unethically violated. To the extent that an organization espouses trust among employees, constructed tags may be incompatible with a larger system of trust.

Fourth, the researcher should identify and access triangulating sources of data when this is possible. As tags move through an organizational process of interest, other sources of information are often suggested. To the extent feasible, the researcher should access these sources. If the hypothetical job candidates in the above example (i.e., the tags) identify inconsistencies in the recruiting system, for instance, the researcher might interview campus recruiters and several actual job candidates for their perceptions regarding these inconsistencies. It should be noted, however, that such subsequent interviews might no longer be feasible, because of violated feelings about trust on the part of the interviewers or insufficient interest among actual job candidates.

Fifth, the researcher must decide upon an end point for the tracer study. If the studied organizational process is well defined, an end point may be readily evident. In the example mentioned above concerning a product's quality control, for instance, the end point becomes apparent when the defective product is identified (or corrected) or when the product moves to shipping. If the studied process is ill defined, the end point should be determined when theoretical saturation is reached (i.e., when additional data collection is judged as likely to lead to no or minimal new learning; see Chapter 3).

Narratives and Life Histories

Because the two techniques are closely interrelated, any distinction drawn between narratives and life histories may be somewhat artificial. I separate them here primarily for ease of discussion. Although part of strong traditions in the humanities (Connelly & Clandinin, 1990; Dollard, 1935), these two methods have not been widely applied in the organizational sciences, thus I discuss them only briefly here. Nonetheless, the potential remains for these techniques to become valued tools for management researchers who must address increasingly controversial social issues.

Narratives. From the traditions of literature, drama, folklore, psychology, and history (Marshall & Rossman, 1995), a narrative describes one or more aspects of an individual's experience. Because a narrative can relate an individual's life's story, the concept of the narrative has some potential overlap with the life history (described below). The creation of a narrative story often relies on such resources as journal records, photographs, letters, and autobiographies to prompt the narrator's recollection of detail. In addition, a narrative is usually created collaboratively between the researcher and narrator. The strengths of this method include a focus on the narrator's interpretations, choice of words, and temporal sequencing. Its weaknesses include potential recall bias and impression management on the part of the narrator, as well as its labor-intensive nature.

Life histories. A life history typically describes how an individual "fits" within a larger culture—whether a larger societal collective or a profession, vocation, or organization. Thus, life histories can help a researcher to understand both socialization and deviance. The strengths of this method include its usefulness in gathering detailed depictions of dynamic processes over a well-defined and meaningful period, because it focuses on a large portion of a life span. Marshall and Rossman (1995, p. 88) describe this strength as allowing the researcher to enter into a "mosaic"; they note that life histories are widely used in feminist studies. The weaknesses involved in the use of life histories include uncertainty about whose histories should be selected, about the generalizability of such histories, and about how to analyze the obtained histories.

Analysis. The verbalized (and transcribed) data gathered through the use of narratives and life histories must be analyzed. The transcribed texts might be analyzed using the methods described in Chapters 3 and 4 (e.g., meaning condensation, meaning categorization, narrative structuring, meaning interpretation, and ad hoc methods). Furthermore, reliability could be readily estimated as well (see Chapter 7).

Comment. Management researchers have unintentionally undervalued the role of rich description in their studies of organizational settings. As a result, their scholarly articles sometimes appear too homogeneous and sanitized. Narratives and life histories can enhance the description of a research site and bring some zest to written reports. In particular, they can enrich, add vividness, and spur insight into other qualitative and quantitative data from organizations. However, the collection of narratives and life histories may require too much detail work from researchers, and so these may not be useful as supplemental techniques. On balance, I believe such techniques are of limited use in organizational studies.

Presentation of Audiovisual Data

Whereas document analysis and construction involves verbal texts, audiovisual data are less well defined and may include any nontext-based materials. Moreover, it can be unclear whether audiovisual data include (a) data collection techniques per se, (b) the collected data themselves, or (c) a neutral medium that houses the data. Nonetheless, a nonexhaustive list of the materials, objects, and topics that can constitute audiovisual data includes photographs, videotapes, art objects, computer software, and films (Creswell, 1995, p. 151). The strengths of the use of audiovisual data include a focus on the subject's perspective and an increase in the likelihood of sustaining the attention of viewers (i.e., consumers of the researcher's end product). The weaknesses of audiovisual data include a potential for ambiguity over interpretation (i.e., invalidity) and invasion of privacy. To date, audiovisual data have seldom been presented in studies in the organizational sciences, thus my discussion of this technique will be brief.

As the traditions of anthropology have shown, films, videos, and photographs can vividly capture and powerfully convey organizational life. Documentaries can strive to be quite literal, depicting specific and contextualized realities. For example, the film *Loose Bolts* dramatically depicts what the filmmaker believed to be actual working conditions, common employee interpretations, and typical managerial actions in a General Motors auto assembly plant in Lordstown, Ohio. Films can also strive to be more figurative, conveying generalized feelings, sentiments, and actions. For instance, the feature film *Roger & Me* humorously presents what the filmmaker believed to be a shared feeling among unemployed General Motors autoworkers.

The greatest strength of the use of film, videotape, and photography may be the potential for deep and long-lasting effects on the viewer through the application of drama, humor, and other strong emotion. Recent reviews of the research on episodic memory, for example, strongly suggest the accuracy of episode-specific recollections (Wheeler, Stuss, & Tulving, 1997). The two greatest weaknesses of audiovisual data lie in the potential for biased presentation (e.g., the filmmaker's selection of materials for inclusion) and the fact that, despite their often powerful nature, these data simply do not lend themselves to presentation in the traditional print-based management journals.

Comment. With the extraordinary advances we have seen in media technology in recent years, a more viable role for audiovisual data may emerge in the near future. Such nontraditional modes of presenting data as film, videotape, and photography will almost certainly become more user-friendly, for example, through low-cost distribution over the Internet, multimedia compact disks, and satellite and laptop computer linkages.

A Nontraditional Example
With the Job Analysis Interview

General Background

In the profession of human resource management, job analysis may be the single most broadly applied analytic technique (Harvey, 1991). Job analysis is conducted for purposes of personnel selection, employee training and development, performance measurement, and compensation administration. Furthermore, job analysis has long been and remains an active topic of research among human resource scholars (Gatewood & Feild, 1994). Because of its ubiquity among human resource practitioners and academics, perhaps, job analysis is seldom considered out of its standard context. It is a basic tool that is routinely applied. As a result, however, job analysis is infrequently inspected. Thus, most human resource scholars and many other management researchers, who tend to be quantitatively oriented, will likely find job analysis an unconventional, if not odd, example to use in a discussion of qualitative methods. Likewise, many qualitatively oriented organizational scientists may find it odd, because job analysis is traditionally considered a quantitative tool. Upon closer examination, job analysis illustrates many of the decisions and techniques routinely practiced by qualitative researchers.

Gatewood and Feild (1994) describe job analysis as "a systematic process for collecting information on the important work-related aspects of the job" (p. 285). Quite commonly, job analysis provides information on the requisite job knowledge, skills, abilities, and performances (or KSAPs) that are necessary to identify, for example, preemployment screening devices and the criteria of job performance against which those screening devices are judged. In addition to their widely accepted role among human resource professionals, job analyses are often necessary parts of a firm's legal defense of its preemployment selection process. In other words, job analysis information is typically required as part of a firm's rebuttal to a charge that it illegally discriminated against an individual. Thus, job analysis is important not only for its role as a basic personnel tool but for its role in litigation as well.

The Job Analysis Interview

Although a host of methods of job analysis exist, the job analysis interview may be the most common form. Ideally, a trained specialist in human resources asks supervisors, job incumbents, peers, and/or subordinates questions about a given job's duties, responsibilities, KSAPs, tools and equipment, conditions of work, and related job categories. These interviews can be unstructured, semistructured, or structured, and may involve individuals or groups. Ideally, the job analyst should be familiar with existing literature (e.g., the U.S. Department of Labor's *Dictionary of Occupational Titles*, 1991, and *Handbook for Analyzing Jobs*, 1972) and interpersonally skilled (e.g., communicative, politically sensitive).

Gatewood and Feild (1994, p. 328) offer the following as typical questions asked during a job analysis interview:

1. *Regarding important job tasks:* Describe your job in terms of what you do. How do you do it? Do you use special tools, equipment, or other sources of aid? Of the major tasks in your job, how much time does it take to do each one? How often do you perform each task in a day, week, or month?
2. *Regarding each important job task:* What does it take to perform each task in terms of job (a) knowledge, (b) skills, and (c) abilities?
3. *Regarding physical abilities:* Describe the frequency and degree to which you engage in such activities as pulling, pushing, throwing, carrying, kneeling, sitting, running, crawling, reaching, climbing?
4. Please describe your typical (a) environmental conditions, (b) work incident report, (c) record keeping and reporting responsibilities, (d) sources of work information, and (e) supervisory responsibilities.

The Job Analyst's Major and Conceptual Qualitative Decisions

Whether conducting a "generic" qualitative research study (see Chapter 2) or employing a long-standing, widely practiced, and legally accepted personnel tool, qualitative organizational researchers and interview-based job analysts must make many decisions and take part in many activities that are quite similar. Both qualitative researchers and job analysts seek to understand how work behaviors are defined, evaluated, and conducted in particular organizational settings. More specifically, both make decisions about the extent to which employees socially construct their organizational worlds, and how they might effectively negotiate (or, from an alternative viewpoint, extract) this information from those worlds. Because in prior chapters I have presented these issues from the qualitative researcher's perspective, in the following discussion I focus on the job analyst's decisions and activities. In particular, the job analyst must make decisions about the extent to which (a) employees engage in the social constructs of their jobs and roles, (b) individuals are affected by their unique perspectives due to their organizational levels, and (c) particular jobs are context dependent.

Jobs and roles. Simultaneously, organizations socialize their members to fit jobs and employees personalize their jobs. In other words, jobs are how organizations structure their employees' work behavior, and roles are how individuals structure their work behaviors (Ilgen & Hollenbeck, 1991). Rarely, however, is there 100% agreement between these structures. To some extent, then, individuals must negotiate and socially construct ("personalize") their job and role domains, and the criteria for their successful performance as well. Through interview-based methods of job analysis, the analyst must decide what constitutes the organizationally constructed "job" versus the individually constructed "role." In other words, the job analyst must meaningfully determine and describe the extent to which social construction occurs.

Organizational level. To the extent that jobs and roles are similarly constructed (e.g., interobserver reliability is high), the job analyst can be less concerned about interviewees' unique perspectives. That is, it matters less whether interviewees are job incumbents, supervisors, peers, or subordinates. They all see, experience, and report on essentially common phenomena. Conversely, to the extent that jobs and roles are dissimilarity constructed (e.g., interobserver agreement is low), the interviewees' perspectives matter. In particular, people at different organizational levels may experience stimuli differently and report on different experiences. Through application of standard methods of job analysis, the analyst must decide what these different persons' experiences with the focal job are and whether these differences really matter. Furthermore, the analyst must meaningfully describe any shared meaning held by individuals at one organizational level and by individuals across different levels as well.

Rich contextualization. In order to function effectively, the job analyst should be aware of and sensitive to the organization's political structures, individuals' hidden agendas, and inter- and intragroup histories. That is, the analyst must thoroughly understand the job's (or role's) contextualizing features and incorporate them into subsequent interpretations of interviewees' comments (e.g., text). Thus, the analyst must fully clarify the dependency between the job (or role) and its context in order to be able to describe the focal job (or role) meaningfully.

The Job Analyst's Major Technical Issues

In addition to making decisions about the extent and meaning of social construction, organizational level, and contextualization, the job analyst must also render and enact decisions about the actual implementation of the investigation. In particular, the analyst must establish rapport with interviewees, select jobs for analysis, and estimate stability of the job's content.

Establishing rapport. From the outset, the job analyst must create a sense of trust and openness with interviewees. He or she may use standard conversational interview techniques, such as courteous introductions, explanation of the interview's purpose, and demonstration of sincere interest in interviewees' responses (see Chapter 4). Regardless of intent, the job analyst must somehow actually achieve positive rapport.

Representatives of jobs and their criticality. In most organizations, jobs fit within a recognizable sequence. In many public accounting firms, for example, many (but certainly not all) entry-level auditors (or associates) advance to the position of manager, but only a smaller subset of these managers become partners. At issue for many job analysts is which jobs should be analyzed. At lower levels, there are many more job incumbents than at higher levels. This larger number of jobholders may mean greater representation of job types, roles, and work behaviors, but it may also imply less criticality. At higher levels, the presence of fewer job incumbents than at lower levels may mean less representativeness, but it may also signal their greater importance.

Stability of job content. In many organizational contexts, job content changes substantially and often because of rapid advances in technology. For example, the drafting of blueprints is today often said to be a lost skill, because most design work is now done directly on computers. The job analyst must monitor and account for the political implications and power changes often associated with changes in technology (or job content) when interpreting interviewees' comments. At issue, then, is whether there is sufficient stability in a job's content and the surrounding political context to make job analysis worthwhile.

Throughout the preceding chapters, I have made frequent reference to and given many specific examples of the blending of quantitative and qualitative analysis. In Chapter 6, discussion turns to the specific quantitative techniques that seem well suited to qualitative studies.

6

Count the Countable

In the course of qualitative research, quantitative data often become available and are (and should be) collected. Typically, these data lend themselves to categorical data analyses. This chapter describes selected tools from the family of techniques for categorical data analysis. First, some situations are presented in which quantitative and qualitative data frequently become available during a single study or across multiple studies within a single stream of research. Then, four indices of association and five types of correlations are discussed. Finally, generalized linear models for slightly more complicated data are briefly described. Throughout the chapter, examples of quantitative tools are presented.

Exemplary Situations for Quantitative and Qualitative Data Collection

In organizational science, both qualitative and quantitative data are often collected within a study or across multiple studies within a single stream of research. In some cases (described in Chapter 1 as two-phase, dominant-less dominant, and mixed-mode designs), researchers intentionally collect both qualitative and quantitative data. Within a case study research design, for instance, my colleagues and I interviewed 44 nurses using a semistructured format (Lee, Mitchell, Wise, & Fireman, 1996). Because the number of cases was "large" by the standards of case

121

study research, we also conducted cross-case statistical analysis with contingency tables, chi-square, log linear modeling, and logistic regressions. Furthermore, human ethnologists, ecological psychologists, and cognitive anthropologists routinely collect qualitative data that they then analyze quantitatively (Marshall & Rossman, 1995).

In other situations, simple opportunity, as well as ambiguities in the empirical findings, can prompt subsequent collection of either quantitative or qualitative data. For example, Sutton and Rafaeli's (1988) widely cited article on displayed emotion has become quite influential. In an unusual trio of essays, Sutton and Rafaeli (1992), Mowday (1992), and Staw (1992) have described how that article came to be. At an early point in their research, Sutton and Rafaeli (1992) say, they thought they "knew our hypothesis was correct and that all they had to do was run the numbers" (p. 120). With what appeared to them to be a "perfect data set" (p. 119), their subsequent ordinary least squares regressions produced results *opposite* to their hypothesis. They were stunned and quite upset (they even avoided each other for a few days; p. 120). At the encouragement of the editor of the *Academy of Management Journal*, however, they explored their phenomena of displayed emotion more deeply with a subsequent qualitative study (Mowday, 1992). After substantial and persistent efforts (Staw, 1992), their ultimately influential, widely cited, and award-winning article was published with both quantitative and qualitative components.

In addition, the analysis of focus group data often involves frequency counts (Morgan, 1997). Sometimes, for example, a given topic's importance is inferred from the number of times it is mentioned during a focus group discussion. In order to corroborate this inferred importance, the researcher simply counts the number of times the topic is mentioned and then makes statistical comparisons among the counts (e.g., chi-square). In turn, the researcher provides feedback on the comparisons to participants, whose subsequent comments can be quite valuable for corroborating a topic's importance as well as clarifying any ambiguities on the researcher's part.

In most survey studies, data are commonly collected using some combination of validated standard scales, unvalidated "armchaired" instruments, and single-item measures (Mangione, 1995). These standard, armchaired, and single-item measures usually produce continuous variables. In my experience, survey researchers are quite confident in their statistical analyses of these continuous data. In other words, they know how to make sense of these data. In some contrast, these same questionnaire studies routinely include open-ended questions (Mangione, 1995). From these open-ended questions, categorical data are almost always produced and content analyzed (e.g., a classification system is imposed on the data). In my discussions with many survey researchers, I have found that they are seldom confident about how they might content analyze and make sense of these categorical data. In many instances data from these open-ended questions are neglected because of the researchers' lack of appropriate techniques.

In sum, organizational researchers often collect both quantitative and qualitative data. Moreover, many of the quantitative data are in the form of nominal or categorical variables. Whereas the analysis of continuous variables is certainly a matter of routine practice, many organizational scientists are less comfortable with analyzing categorical data. This discomfort may be particularly acute among more qualitatively oriented researchers, in part because their quantitative data usually derive from relatively small sample sizes. Nevertheless, researchers should try not to miss any researcher-created or serendipitous opportunities to glean more information from their quantitative (or qualitative) data.

The next section presents some techniques for documenting statistical associations among categorical variables that may be collected during a qualitative study: relative risks, odds ratios, cross-product ratio, and chi-squares. These indices are most often applied when sample sizes are small. Derivations are not presented here, because it is my intent for the remainder of this chapter to be conversational in nature; however, some use of symbols, formula-like notation, and conceptual formulas is un-avoidable. For excellent discussions on the application of these and other indices, see Guilford and Fruchter (1973) for an introductory treatment and Agresti (1990, 1996) for more advanced treatment.

Associations Between
Two Categorical Variables

Nominal and Categorical Variables

Qualitative researchers often study the nature of some kind of (an organizational) phenomenon (Kvale, 1996). That is, they tend to focus and gather data on the presence or absence of the components of that phenomenon. Although I have mentioned them throughout this book, I have not specifically defined nominal and categorical variables.

In its simplest form, the term *nominal variable* refers to the presence or absence of some state or condition. It is the simplest and binary form of categorical conditions. In other words, the organizational phenomenon of interest is either present or absent. For example, employee turnover is most often taken to be a "truly" dichotomous variable (Hom & Griffeth, 1995). An employee is either employed or formerly employed, and employment is the "thing, condition, or state" that is either present or absent. Typically, operationalization of employee turnover occurs with a former employee coded as one and a current employee coded as zero.

Whereas all nominal variables are categorical, not all categorical variables are nominal. In addition to binary conditions, other categorical variables include multiple states. The organizational phenomenon of interest can occur as one of several possible states (or conditions). For instance, although it can be binary, employee absenteeism is usually defined as multicategorical. Common absence categories include certified medical illness; certified accident, either work related or domestic; contractual absence, such as jury duty, bereavement, or union activities; disciplinary suspension; and "other" (Rhodes & Steers, 1990). Conceptually, these categories can be further collapsed into measures of magnitude, occurrence, and duration. Operationally, these multiple categories are often captured with dummy variables or effect codes (Cohen & Cohen, 1983).

Describing the Association
Between Two Categorical Variables

In the simplest case, interest may focus on describing the strength of association between two categorical variables. In this section, I use gender and turnover as a running example. In the initial structuring of these data, a contingency table would almost certainly be constructed early on.

Contingency tables. As illustrated in Table 6.1, a 2 × 2 contingency table cross-tabulates the data on gender and turnover as follows. For each case or person, occurrence or nonoccurrence of the phenomenon of interest is recorded. Typically, nonoccurrence is coded as zero and occurrence is coded as one. In each cell, these observed occurrences are recorded and

TABLE 6.1 A 2 × 2 Contingency Table: Turnover Cross-Tabulated With Gender

Turnover	Gender		Total
	Males	*Females*	*Total*
Employed	no. counted = a (cell 1)	no. counted = b (cell 2)	$(a + b)$
Formerly employed	no. counted = c (cell 3)	no. counted = d (cell 4)	$(c + d)$
Total	$(a + c)$	$(b + d)$	$(a + b + c + d) = T$

summed. In the example in Table 6.1, cell 1 (row 1, column 1) has a total of a employed males, cell 2 (row 1, column 2) has a total of b employed females, cell 3 (row 2, column 1) has a total of c formerly employed males, and cell 4 (row 2, column 2) has a total of d formerly employed females. T is the grand total (or overall) number of observations based on $a + b + c + d$.

Proportions, probabilities, and successes. For each cell in Table 6.1, the number of observed cases (or persons) can be divided by the total number of cases (or persons). These proportions are the probabilities for the occurrence of the phenomenon of interest defined by each cell. In this example, the following probabilities exist: of finding an employed male (cell 1), $p = a/T$; of finding an employed female (cell 2), $p = b/T$; of finding a formerly employed male (cell 3), $p = c/T$; and of finding a formerly employed female (cell 4), $p = d/T$. For each row or column, the number of cases (or persons) can also be divided by its corresponding total. These proportions are the probabilities for the occurrence of the phenomenon of interest defined by each row or column. In this example, these probabilities are as follows: of finding an employed person (cells 1 and 2), $p = (a + b)/T$; of finding a formerly employed person (cells 3 and 4), $p = (c + d)/T$; of finding a male (cells 1 and 3), $p = (a + c)/T$; and of finding a female (cells 2 and 4), $p = (b + d)/T$. In the jargon of statistics, these probabilities of occurrences (e.g., employed male or formerly employed female) are also called *successes*.

Relative risks. When interest focuses on describing or comparing two probabilities of success (i.e., the occurrence of some phenomenon of interest, such as being employed or being unemployed), their relative risk is often calculated. Simply put, the relative risk is the ratio of their successes, or, alternatively stated, the ratio of their probabilities of occurrences. For example, the relative risk of finding an employed person versus an unemployed person is $[(a + b)/T]$ divided by $[(c + d)/T]$. Relative risk is particularly useful when both successes (or probabilities) are close to either zero or one, because their relative magnitudes can be substantial at those ranges. Thus, if an organizational researcher wants to quantify the categorical observations of employed versus unemployed (or male versus female), the ratio of risks is conceptually simple and easy to compute. Depending upon sample size and the assumptions about the population the researcher is willing to make, calculation of relative risks also lends itself to different sampling distributions and confidence intervals for the purposes of testing statistical significance (Agresti, 1996).

Odds ratio. Whereas relative risk describes a ratio of probabilities, the odds ratio describes the ratio of two odds. In other words, the odds ratio might be calculated when the researcher's interest focuses on the odds of events, which is frequently the statistician's index of choice. The odds of an event can be defined as the probability of that event's occurring (e.g., being employed) divided by the probability that the event does *not* occur (e.g., one minus being employed). From Table 6.1, the odds of being employed are $[(a + b)/T]$ divided by $[1 - (a + b)/T]$. Similarly, the odds of being unemployed can be calculated as $[(c + d/T]$ divided by $[1 - (c + d)/T]$. The odds ratio is simply the ratio of those two odds, or $\{[(a + b)/T]$ divided by $[1 - (a + b)/T]\}$ divided by $\{[(c + d/T]$ divided by $[1 - (c + d/T]\}$.

Cross-products ratio. The odds ratio is more widely used than relative risk. In part, this may be the case because the odds ratio is a basic building block for more advanced methods of categorical data analysis, which may explain why it is often the statistician's index of choice. Another reason for its wider use may be its ease of calculation. The odds ratio is sometimes called the cross-products ratio because of the following property. From the prior contingency table, the odds ratio equals (a/c) divided by (b/d), which equals $(a \times d)/(c \times b)$. In words, the total number of occurrences from cell 1 is first multiplied by the total number from cell 4; the total number from cell 3 is next multiplied by the total number from cell 2; and third, the two resulting multiplicative products are then divided to obtain the odds ratio. Values of the odds ratio that are *near* one imply minimal association (or independence between the two rows); values that are *below* one imply a negative association (or a success is less likely in row 1 than in row 2); and values that are *above* one imply a positive association (or a success is more likely in row 1 than in row 2). Like relative risk, the odds ratio also lends itself to different sampling distributions and confidence intervals for the purposes of testing statistical significance, depending upon sample size and the assumptions about the population the researcher is willing to make (Agresti, 1996). As a rule of thumb, nevertheless, values of the odds (or cross-products) ratio that are greater than 2 are sometimes taken to be "meaningful."

Testing the Association Between Two
Categorical Variables With Chi-Squares

The most common statistical test for an association between two categorical variables may be chi-square. In particular, chi-square can be used to answer such questions as, Do the data show that the two categorical variables are associated beyond a chance level? Referring to Table 6.1, alternatively asked questions include the following: Does being employed depend upon an individual's gender? Is employment status correlated to gender? Is frequency of employment the same for men and women?

General model. An extraordinarily useful property of chi-square is that the sum of chi-squares equals another chi-square. As such, the chi-squares from each cell of a contingency table sum to a larger chi-square. The general form of chi-square is

$$\chi^2 = E(f_{observed} - f_{expected})^2 / f_{expected}$$

where E stands for "sum of" across cells, $f_{observed}$ stands for an observed frequency (or cell total; e.g., cell 1 from Table 6.1), and $f_{expected}$ stands for an expected frequency. In the specialized case of contingency tables, including a 2×2, a general form for the expected frequency of any cell is

$$f_{\text{expected (rk)}} = f_r f_k / N,$$

where f stands for frequency, r stands for row, and k stands for column. In words, one would do the following:

1. Count the f_{observed} and f_{expected} for each cell.
2. Subtract the expected from the corresponding observed frequencies for each cell (i.e., $f_{\text{observed}} - f_{\text{expected}}$).
3. Square these amounts for each cell (i.e., $[f_{\text{observed}} - f_{\text{expected}}]^2$).
4. Sum the squared values (i.e., $E[f_{\text{observed}} - f_{\text{expected}}]^2$).
5. Divide these squared amounts by expected frequencies (i.e., $[E(f_{\text{observed}} - f_{\text{expected}})^2 / f_{\text{expected}}$).

The calculated chi-square value could then be compared to a "critical value" from a chi-square distribution to test for the statistical significance of an association between two categorical variables.

Yates's correction. When (a) samples sizes are below 10, (b) count (or frequency) data are involved, and (c) there is only a single degree of freedom, Yates's "correction for continuity" should be applied to the calculation of chi-square (Guilford & Fruchter, 1973). This correction subtracts or adds a value to each observed cell. More specifically, it adjusts the cell count by $-.5$ when the difference between the observed frequency is *greater* than the expected frequency and by $+.5$ when the difference between the observed frequency is *less* than the expected frequency. Yates's correction serves to equate chi-square when it is based on discrete instead of continuous data.

Degrees of freedom. In the application of chi-square to a 2×2 contingency table (such as that shown in Table 6.1), the general rule is that there is one degree of freedom (*df*). For example, $df = (r - 1)(k - 1)$, where r is the number of rows and k is the number of columns. In words, a 2×2 contingency table has four marginal totals: $(a + b)$, $(c + d)$, $(a + c)$, and $(b + d)$. When any one of the four cell totals (i.e., *a, b, c,* or *d*) has been observed (or counted), the remaining three cell totals become mathematically determined (or known).

Correlation Involving One
or Two Categorical Variables

Pearson Product-Moment Correlation

Perhaps all organizational researchers are familiar with the Pearson product-moment correlation (r). It is a single number that describes how two continuous variables are related. Specifically, r indexes the changes in one variable systematically associated with changes in another. Moreover, it is so prevalent and robustly applicable in organizational science that the r may (and should) be calculated as part of virtually every initial analysis of a quantitative data set, even when it is less appropriate in a particular analytic situation. Nonetheless, ease of calculation and its robustness certainly justify use of r during any first, "rough-cut" look at the data.

At more advanced stages of analysis, particularly when interest involves categorical variables, r may not fit the analytic situation and should not be used or appear in a research report. Because qualitative researchers often collect categorical data, it is likely that they would need to use better-suited forms of correlation than r, particularly in later stages of data analysis. In my judgment, organizational researchers should use these alternative forms of correlation during these later stages and report them when appropriate.

Below, I discuss five less well-known forms of correlation: Spearman's rho, biserial correlation, point-biserial correlation, tetrachoric correlation, and phi coefficients. It should be noted that none of these involves two continuous variables, which is the analytic situation best suited for the Pearson product-moment correlation.

Spearman's Rho

Two ranked variables. Sometimes, interest focuses on rank orderings. These data can be rank orderings themselves or continuous variables that were converted to ranks (particularly when sample sizes are small). In such cases, Spearman's rank difference correlation may be appropriate. For example, five (or perhaps many more) individuals might rank order their preferences for a set of 10 (real or paper-profile) job candidates. Most directly, the rank orderings of any pair from these five individuals could be correlated with rho. Alternatively, each of the 10 job candidates might be ranked based on a reverse scoring of the assigned rankings (e.g., each first-place ranking would earn 10 points, each second-place ranking would earn 9 points, each third-place ranking would earn 8 points, and so on). In turn, each job candidate could then be rank ordered based on his or her total number of points). These converted ranks could also be correlated with rho.

General model. The general form of rho is

$$rho = 1 - [(6ED^2)/N(N^2 - 1)],$$

where E stands for "sum of," D stands for the difference between each pair of rankings, and N stands for the number of pairs. In words, one would do the following:

1. Calculate the differences between each pair of rankings (i.e., D).
2. Square each of those values (i.e., D^2).
3. Sum across those squared values (i.e., ED^2) and multiply that sum by six (i.e., $6 \times ED^2$) to obtain the numerator.
4. Square the number of pairs (i.e., N^2) and subtract one from that squared value (i.e., $N^2 - 1$).
5. Multiply the resulting value by N (i.e., $N[N^2 - 1]$) to obtain the denominator.
6. Divide the numerator by the denominator.
7. Subtract the resulting fraction from one.

Standard error. Guilford and Fruchter (1973) indicate that there is no accepted standard error formula for Spearman's rho. As a result, confidence intervals cannot be readily calculated. To test rho against the null hypothesis of "no difference from zero," however, a standard error can be obtained as follows:

$$SE = 1/\sqrt{(N - 1)}.$$

When sample size is 25 or more, and there is no reason *not* to assume a normal parent population, a normal sampling distribution can be assumed. When sample size is smaller than 25, a sampling distribution specifically tailored to Spearman's rho should be used.

Comment. Spearman's rho was designed to estimate r. It is not itself a form of r, however. Nonetheless, and broadly speaking, rho produces values that are very close to r on the unranked data. Thus, one can be quite confident in the estimates for rho.

Biserial Correlation

One artificially dichotomized variable and one continuous variable. On occasion, interest focuses on estimating the relationship between a continuous variable that has been dichotomized for some reason and another continuous variable. Under these conditions, a biserial correlation (r_b) can be appropriate. For example, a corporation's information system may only record applicants' "pass-fail" status on a preemployment physical abilities test. In contrast, it may also record their actual scores from a standard test of general mental abilities. Thus, data are "artificially dichotomized" on the physical abilities test, whereas they are "complete" on the general mental abilities test. Because of the information system's configuration, analyzable and potentially useful information from the physically abilities test has been lost. Nonetheless, artificially dichotomized continuous variables are often unavoidable because much of qualitative research involves searches of archival records and other such data.

General model. Although there are many computational models for biserial correlation, its basic logic is that a relationship is indicated by a mean difference on the continuous variable (e.g., general mental abilities) *when* individuals (or other entities) are grouped by the artificially dichotomized variable (e.g., physical abilities). One computational model is as follows:

$$r_b = [(M_p - M_t)/SD_t] \times [pq/y],$$

where M_p refers to the mean of the group with more of the continuous variable (e.g., physical abilities), M_t refers to mean of the total sample on the continuous variable, SD_t refers to the standard deviation from the entire sample on the continuous variable, p refers to the proportion of cases (or individuals) from the higher group, and y refers to the ordinate of the standard normal distribution at the point between segments containing p and q (i.e., proportion of cases from the lower group). In words, one would do the following:

1. Calculate the means for the total sample (M_t) and the p group (M_p) on the continuous variable.
2. Subtract M_t from M_p.
3. Calculate the standard deviation of the continuous variable (SD_t) from the entire sample.
4. Divide the value from Step 2 by SD_t, which produces the left side of the equation.
5. Count p and q.
6. Determine y from a table of normal distribution values.
7. Multiply p by q and divide pq by y.
8. Multiply the values from Steps 4 and 7.

Standard error. To test the null hypothesis of "no difference from zero," a standard error can be determined by $\sqrt{(pq)}/(y\sqrt{N})$. Guilford and Fruchter (1973) warn that p and q must both exceed a value of .05 for this estimate of the standard error to hold.

Comment. Biserial correlations were derived to estimate Pearson's product-moment correlation. Thus, they are not themselves a form of *r*. Nonetheless, when both variables can be taken as normally distributed, r_b can produce good approximations of *r*. However, biserial correlations appear to be quite sensitive to departures from normality. Thus, r_b can result in quite poor estimates of *r* as well. Unless the researcher is confident in making assumptions about the normality of the two underlying continuous variables, he or she would be well-advised to provide clear warnings about the accuracy of r_b.

Point-Biserial Correlation

One true dichotomous variable and one continuous variable. Often, interest focuses on estimating the relationship between a variable accepted as truly dichotomous (e.g., employee turnover) and another continuous variable (e.g., job satisfaction). In such a case, a point-biserial correlation (r_{pb}) may be most appropriate. Point-biserial correlation is derived from Pearson's product-moment correlation, and is therefore a special case of r.

General model. Although there are many computational models for point-biserial correlation, its basic logic is similar to that of the biserial correlation. That is, a relationship is indicated by a mean difference on the continuous variable (e.g., job satisfaction) when grouped by the truly (instead of artificially) dichotomized variable (e.g., employee turnover). One computational model is as follows:

$$r_{pb} = [(M_p - M_t)/SD_t] \times \sqrt{(p/q)},$$

where M_p refers to the mean of the group with more of the continuous variable (e.g., job satisfaction), M_t refers to mean of the total sample on the continuous variable, SD_t refers to the standard deviation from the entire sample on the continuous variable, p refers to the proportion of cases (or individuals) from the higher group, and q refers to the proportion of cases (or individuals) from the lower group. In words, one would do the following:

1. Calculate the means for the total sample (M_t) and the p group (M_p) on the continuous variable.
2. Subtract M_t from M_p (i.e., $M_p - M_t$).
3. Calculate the standard deviation of the continuous variable (SD_t) for the entire sample.
4. Divide the value from Step 2 by SD_t, which produces the left side of the equation (i.e., $M_p - M_t/SD_t$).
5. Count p and q.
6. Divide p by q and take the result's square root (i.e., $\sqrt{p/q}$).
7. Multiply the values from Steps 4 and 6.

Significance of point-biserial correlation. To test the null hypothesis of "no difference from zero," a *t* test should be calculated on the means for the p and q groups (i.e., M_p and M_q). A significant *t* statistic indicates a significant r_{pb}, whereas a nonsignificant *t* statistic indicates no relationship.

Comment. It should be noted that when the proportions of cases in each group formed by the dichotomous variable are equal (i.e., p = q), r_{pb} will closely approximate *r*. As the proportions of cases in the groups formed by the dichotomous variables increasingly differ (e.g., p < q or p > q), r_{pb} will approximate *r* less well. Furthermore, sometimes researchers have difficulty choosing between point-biserial and biserial correlations. It is often difficult, for example, to decide whether a binary variable is a true or artificial dichotomy. Presuming *r* is clearly inappropriate and some ambiguity over whether the dichotomous variable is true or artificial, the point-biserial correlation should be selected over the biserial correlation because r_{pb} is a more accurate estimator than r_b. Thus, unless conditions clearly suggest biserial correlation (e.g., normally distributed but artificially dichotomized continuous variables), r_{pb} is usually preferable.

Tetrachoric Correlation

Two artificially dichotomized variables. Similar to conditions suggesting a biserial correlation, interest sometimes focuses on the relationship between two continuous variables that have been artificially dichotomized. Under these conditions, a tetrachoric correlation (r_t) may be appropriate. For example, job satisfaction and income are most often considered continuous variables. On occasion, both variables are recorded simply as high versus low. Possible reasons for these artificial splits include saving computer space, easing the variables' measurement, and pre-existing bias toward simplicity.

General model. Although there are many computational formulas, a relatively uncomplicated version is as follows:

$$r_t = \cos[(180 \text{ degrees})/(1 + \sqrt{ad/bc})],$$

where cos refers to cosine; 180 degrees refers to a geometric angle; and *a, b, c,* and *d* refer to the cells from a 2 × 2 contingency table formed by the four groups from the two dichotomized variables (e.g., see Table 6.1).

Standard error. To test the null hypothesis of "no difference from zero," a standard error can be determined by $\sqrt{(p_1 p_2 q_1 q_2)}/y_1 y_2 \sqrt{N}$, where p_1 stands for the proportion of cases (or individuals) from the higher group in variable 1, p_2 stands for the proportion of cases (or individuals) from the higher group in variable 2, q_1 stands for the proportion of cases (or individuals) from the lower group in variable 1, q_2 stands for the proportion of cases (or individuals) from the lower group in variable 2, y_1 stands for the ordinate of the standard normal distribution at the point between segments containing p_1 and q_1, and y_2 stands for the ordinate of the standard normal distribution at the point between segments containing p_2 and q_2.

Comment. Three issues merit brief comment. First, tetrachoric correlations were derived to estimate Pearson's product-moment correlation; they are not themselves a form of r. Nonetheless, when both variables can be taken as normally distributed, r_t can produce good approximations of r. Like biserial correlations, however, tetrachoric correlations appear to be quite sensitive departures from normality. As such, r_t can also result in quite poor estimates of r as well. Second, somewhat like the point-biserial correlation, r_t best approximates r when the proportions of cases in the groups formed by both dichotomous variables are approximately equal (i.e., $p_1 = q_1$ and $p_2 = q_2$). As the proportions of cases in any of the groups formed by the dichotomous variables differ (e.g., $p_1 < q_1$ or $p_2 > q_2$), r_t will approximate r less well. Third, r_t is less reliable than r because of lower variability in the two artificially dichotomized variables. Like all correlations, r_t is most reliable when (a) sample size is large and (b) their underlying relationship is quite strong. Because of this large sample size constraint, however, r_t may not be well suited to qualitative research, and should be used with care.

Phi Coefficients

Two true dichotomous variables. Often, interest focuses on the relationship between two variables accepted as truly dichotomous. Recall, for example, the presentation of gender and employee turnover in Table 6.1. Both variables are widely taken as true dichotomies. In such a case, phi coefficients may be appropriate. It might be noted that, like the point-biserial correlation, phi is also a special case of Pearson's product-moment correlation. Thus, its values can be similarly interpreted. In this section, Table 6.1 can be used as a running example.

Model for a 2 × 2 contingency table. In the specialized case of the 2 × 2 contingency table, phi can be obtained as follows:

$$\text{phi} = [(ad) - (bc)] / \sqrt{(a + b)(a + c)(b + d)(c + d)},$$

where *a* is the frequency from cell 1 (row 1, column 1), *b* is the frequency from cell 2 (row 1, column 2), *c* is the frequency from cell 3 (row 2, column 1), and *d* is the frequency from cell 4 (row 2, column 2).

Significance for phi. To test the null hypothesis of "no difference from zero," one can rely on the conceptual dependence between phi and chi-square. In particular, $\text{phi} = \sqrt{\chi^2/N}$; alternatively, $\chi^2 = N(\text{phi})^2$. As such, when chi-square is statistically significant, the corresponding phi is also significant.

Comment. Sometimes researchers have difficulty in choosing between phi coefficients and tetrachoric correlations. It can be difficult, for instance, to decide whether a binary variable is a true or artificial dichotomy. Presuming *r* is clearly inappropriate and some ambiguity over whether the dichotomous variables are true or artificial, the phi coefficient should be selected over the tetrachoric correlation because phi is a more accurate estimator than r_t. Thus, unless conditions clearly suggest tetrachoric correlation (e.g., normally distributed but artificially dichotomized continuous variables), phi is usually preferable.

Modeling Associations With Categorical, Continuous, or Both Kinds of Variables

The two most common techniques that fall into this category are log linear modeling and logistic regression. Other potential techniques include probit regression and discriminant analysis, but these are not as frequently seen anymore. In my experience, applications of log linear modeling and logistic regressions can be quite complicated. Because three or (usually) more variables are typically involved, many applications require substantial sample sizes (e.g., 10 cases per included variable). As a result, the applicability of log linear modeling and logistic regression to the quantitative data commonly collected during a qualitative study is likely to be somewhat limited. Thus, I describe these techniques below, but only briefly. In particular, my focus is more on specifying the conditions under which these techniques might be useful, and less on how to conduct these analyses. Readers who believe they might find these techniques useful are referred to the sources cited below.

As far as I know, there are no "simple" treatments of these two techniques. For intermediate-level discussion of log linear modeling, DeMaris (1992) and Hout (1983) are excellent sources and quite readable. For intermediate-level discussion of logistic (and probit) regression, Aldrich and Nelson (1984) and Menard (1995) are excellent sources, as well as quite readable. For advanced discussions, see Agresti (1990, 1996) on log linear modeling and logistic regression and see Hosmer and Lemeshow (1989) on applications of logistic regression. Although excellent treatments, these latter three sources can be challenging to read.

Log Linear Models

Thus far, discussion in this chapter has focused on associations and correlations between two variables, and categorical variables have been restricted to the binary condition. However, research interest can often involve three or more categorical variables, rendering the prior discussion moot. Log linear models allow for the documentation of associations among (a) two or more categorical variables, with each variable including (b) two or more categorical states. Note, however, that log linear models cannot include continuous variables. If continuous variables must be involved, logistic (or probit) regression should be used.

Technically, log linear models do not differ between dependent and independent variables. Instead, all associations among all variables are modeled and potentially interpretable. By interpreting some and not other associations, however, the researcher can impose the de facto designations of dependent and independent variables.

Recall the example depicted in Table 6.1, where employee turnover is crossed with gender. Suppose, for instance, that a third categorical dimension were added: race. For the sake of simplicity, race is limited to Black, White, and Asian. Thus, the corresponding contingency table becomes three-dimensional and can be depicted by a 2 (employed, unemployed) × 2 (men, women) × 3 (Black, White, Asian) lopsided cube.

The previously discussed techniques can establish an association between any two of these three variables. However, those techniques (i.e., relative risks, odds and cross-product ratios, chi-square, and phi coefficients) do not allow for control of the effects from the third variable. In comparison, log linear models allow for the simultaneous documentation of associations among all three variables and between any two variables, while holding the effects of the third variable constant. To draw an analogy: The previously discussed pair-based techniques are to log linear modeling what *t* tests are to the analysis of variance.

The modeled entity. In log linear modeling, the modeled entity is the expected frequency count of any given cell from a contingency table. This expected count can be expressed as a number, a probability, or an odds. Most commonly, the modeled entity is the *logarithm (or log) of an odds.* Although two- and three-way tables are discussed here, the principles of log linear modeling easily generalize to any *n*-way table (in *n*-dimensional space). Thus, the expected log odds for employed Black men (or any other cell) can be expressed as a log linear model, and the associations among any combination of employment, gender, and race can be documented. Note that the particular cell that is log linear modeled is far less important than the dependent variable from a typical regression equation. The primary function of the modeled cell is to allow for subsequent calculation of that model's parameters. It is important to note that these parameters hold the analyses' substantive information.

Parameters. A log linear model derives from the larger family of generalized linear models. Thus, its parts are analogous to those of analysis of variance, which is also a member of this larger family of models. In log linear models, the main parameters are (a) a *grand mean*, which is an average expected log frequency over all cells in a contingency table; (b) *main effects*, which are the effects due to row (e.g., turnover), column (e.g., gender), and additional *n* dimensions (e.g., race); and, most important, (c) the *interactions*, which provide the substantive information about one or more statistical associations among categorical variables. As in analysis of variance, the grand mean and main effects must be present in the log linear model, but they are not directly interpretable. Like their analogous parts in analysis of variance, they are, instead, "necessary" components that allow for the subsequent calculation and interpretation of the interaction parameters. For example, a two-way log linear model has two main effects (e.g., a row and column) that cannot be directly interpreted and a single two-way interaction (e.g., row × column) that provides information directly on whether these two categorical variables represented by the row and column are associated (e.g., turnover and gender). In other words, the coefficient for the interaction term indicates whether there is an association between the two categorical variables. A three-way log linear model has three main effects (e.g., turnover, gender, race), three two-way interactions (e.g., turnover-gender, gender-race, turnover-race), and a single three-way interaction (e.g., turnover-gender-race). Each interaction has a coefficient that can be statistically tested and interpreted for the presence of an association.

Comment. As in analysis of variance, each added categorical variable quickly increases the number of possible *n*-way interactions. Given the typically small samples found in qualitative research, the number of included variables in a log linear model must be kept small. Thus, very careful discretion must be exercised in the choice of analyzed variables.

Logistic Regression

Whereas log linear models do not formally specify a dependent variable and are limited to categorical variables, most research questions in organizational science specify a formal outcome variable of interest and some combination of categorical and continuous predictors. Moreover, researcher interest typically moves beyond the search for associations between or among categorical variables. Analogous to the widely known ordinary least squares (OLS) linear regression (Cohen & Cohen, 1983), most research questions in the organizational sciences involve either (a) *modeling* a set of categorical, continuous, or some combination of both these kinds of predictor variables or (b) *predicting* some outcome of interest (e.g., employee turnover). (The discussion that follows presumes that the reader has some familiarity with OLS regression.)

Under most conditions involving modeling or predicting, OLS regression is the most natural, powerful, and flexible tool for analysis. In particular, OLS regression should almost certainly be applied if (a) the sample size is sufficiently large (e.g., 10 cases per predictor variable), (b) the dependent variable is continuous, and (c) the corresponding error terms are normally distributed (with mean of zero and standard deviation of one).

With qualitative data, however, the dependent variable is often dichotomous in nature (e.g., appropriate versus inappropriate dress in the workplace; Pratt & Rafaeli, 1997). With this added condition of a binary outcome variable of interest, OLS regression simply becomes inappropriate because (a) the predicted dependent variable often assumes undefined values (e.g., greater than one or less than zero) and (b) the error terms cannot be distributed normally. As a result, these violations to the assumptions underlying OLS regression preclude its application as an inferential statistical technique (e.g., hypothesis testing or construction of confidence intervals).

With a binary dependent variable, logistic regression has emerged as the alternative technique of choice. Analogous to OLS regression, logistic regression can (a) *model* a set of predictor variables and (b) *predict* a dichotomous dependent variable of interest. Unlike OLS regression, it allows for inferential statistics, such as hypothesis testing or construction of confidence intervals. Moreover, with the exception of the dependent variable itself, the rest of the logistic regression equation resembles that of virtually any other general linearized model. (Logistic regression is itself simply another version of the generalized linear model.)

Recall the example in Table 6.1, where employee turnover is crossed by gender. Furthermore, recall the expanded version above, a lopsided cube depicting employee turnover crossed by gender, and both turnover and gender crossed by race. Add to this $2 \times 2 \times 3$ design the continuous variable job satisfaction. (Geometric representations become impossible at this point.) If employee turnover is designated the dependent variable and gender, race, and job satisfaction are designated the predictor variables, this emergent analytic situation calls for a logistic regression model.

For these hypothetical data, the prior techniques of categorical data analysis are inappropriate. Log linear modeling is inappropriate because of the addition of the continuous variable, job satisfaction. It might be recalled that designation of a dependent variable does not by itself preclude use of log linear models. In addition, OLS regression is inappropriate because of the binary dependent variable. However, the correlational techniques discussed above are somewhat appropriate. Because they deal only with two variables at a time, however, they do not control for the effects of additional variables (e.g., the third and fourth predictors); thus, they would be inefficient.

The simple logistic regression model. In the simple case, there is one binary dependent variable (e.g., employee turnover) and one predictor variable (e.g., job satisfaction). The corresponding logistic regression can be written as

$$\log\{\pi(x)/[1 - \pi(x)]\} = a + Bx,$$

where $\pi(x)$ stands for the probability of x and $\pi(x)/[1 - \pi(x)]$ is an odds ratio. (This first formula implies that the logistic regression has an S-shaped curve; Agresti, 1996.) Note that in logistic regression, the predicted binary dependent variable is transformed into the *log of an odds*, and it appears on the left side of the equation. On the right side of the equation, the regression model appears similar to virtually any generalized linear model. Alternatively, the logistic regression can be written as

$$\pi(x) = \exp(a + Bx)/[1 + \exp(a + Bx)],$$

which simply moves the logging from the left side of the equation to the right side through introduction of exponential notation. In a somewhat more intuitive form, the logistic regression can be written as

$$[\pi(x)/[1 - \pi(x)] = \exp(a + Bx) = (e^{a})(e^{B})^{x},$$

which offers a specific meaning for the regression coefficient, B. That is, the exponential relationship says that the odds of the event of interest (e.g., employee turnover) increase multiplicatively by e^{B} for every unit increase in x (e.g., job satisfaction). Thus, in applying (or estimating) this simple logistic regression model, antilogging must be conducted before a specific interpretation of B is made. (Very few management researchers likely hold a worldview or organizational view in log form.)

Multiple logistic regression. Analogous to OLS regression, the simple case generalizes to the multiple predictor case. For example, we might view this chapter's running example as "Employee turnover is a function of gender, race, and job satisfaction," and it might depicted as follows:

$$\text{Employee Turnover} = f(\text{Gender, Race, Job Satisfaction}).$$

Alternatively, and correspondingly stated, the relationship might expressed as

$$Y = f(X_1, X_2, X_3).$$

In terms of a logistic regression, the relationship would be expressed as

$$\text{logit}(\pi) = a + B_1X_1 + B_2X_2 + B_3X_3,$$

where π stands for employee turnover, X_1 stands for gender, X_2 stands for race, and X_3 stands for job satisfaction. Note that logistic regression expresses units in terms of logs and odds. Because these terms are not common to everyday understanding, researchers should convert these obtained values to natural numbers before attempting any substantive interpretation (i.e., antilogging).

Comment. As in OLS regression, confidence intervals for parameter estimates can be constructed. Tests for the statistical significance of intercepts and the regression coefficients for predictor variables and their interaction terms can be easily conducted. Even model checking can be calculated. Although logistic regression is quite flexible and powerful, the fact that it may require a substantial sample size should not be overlooked. Thus, researchers must exercise care in their choice of included variables.

Conclusion

The topics in this chapter have continued the overall trend from the more general conceptual ideas described in earlier chapters (e.g., What is qualitative research?) to very specific applications (e.g., What is a logistic regression, and when does it apply?). However, the main point of this chapter should not be lost among its quantitative detail. Specifically, qualitative researchers should *always* follow Cassell and Symon's (1994) advice to "count the countable." In virtually every qualitative study, opportunities arise for the researcher to collect at least some quantitative data. Unfortunately, these opportunities are often ignored or the data underutilized. As a result, meaningful information is likely missed. Given the high cost of collecting virtually any organizational data, such omission is simply too costly.

7   The Cardinal Concepts of Reliability and Validity

This chapter first reviews the traditional concepts of reliability and validity, and then discusses the approaches to reliability and validity taken by several qualitative methodologists. Several themes from these reviews are identified, and specific tactics that are often useful in demonstrating the reliability and validity of studies are noted. The chapter concludes with the observation that the concepts of reliability and validity have broad applicability to qualitative research and a recommendation that these concepts be formally addressed in all qualitative research reports. Throughout the chapter, the author's opinions are offered.

Conceptualization and Measurement in the Organizational Sciences

In the larger world of social science, conceptualization and measurement of economic, sociological, and psychological constructs are universally accepted as playing key roles in the judgment of the quality of research (Blalock, 1982; Nunnally, 1978). In the smaller world of organizational science, the closely related ideas of reliability and validity have been similarly accepted as critical to the evaluation of research (Schwab, 1980). Although management researchers consider the concepts of reliability and validity to be important, there is a very real dichotomy between qualitative and quantitative researchers in how they apply these concepts. It often appears that these ideas, though universally recognized as valuable, are taken to be less important when the issue is the evaluation of actual qualitative research. Some qualitative researchers argue, for instance, that traditional notions of reliability and validity do not readily apply to their studies, and that it is often inappropriate to try to apply them. In contrast, many quantitative, as well as many qualitative, researchers view such assertions with skepticism. However, because many quantitative researchers have insufficient familiarity with qualitative methods, they cannot forcefully rebut these claims. It has long been my opinion that this insufficient familiarity contributes to the tensions often felt between the quantitative and qualitative camps.

Although the traditions of qualitative and quantitative research certainly differ, I would argue that the ideas of reliability and validity apply equally well to both. Any study's conceptualizations, measurement processes, and interpretations should be chosen carefully and systematically, and should be *representative* of the phenomena of interest. The clarification of the utility of these concepts is critical to the expansion of the application of qualitative research in organizational science and to the blending of qualitative and quantitative designs. My goal in this chapter is to provide that clarification.

Traditional Views on Reliability

In its simplest meaning, *reliability* refers to the consistency and stability of "scores." These scores are assumed to result from some "measurement process." *Consistency* is most often thought to mean repeatability. If one were to replicate a certain hypothetical measurement process numerous times, for example, consistency would be demonstrated if the obtained scores occurred within some acceptable margin of error. *Stability* is most often thought to mean the obtained scores' consistency over time. Furthermore, these scores can represent a continuous, finely calibrated, and random variable (e.g., job satisfaction). Alternatively, these scores can represent the presence or absence of some categorical state, condition, or class (e.g., a CEO's staying or leaving). Between continuous and dichotomous variables, scores can also represent the ordering of categorical states (e.g., employees' salaries arranged in increments of $10,000). The measurement process can take the form of a standard, off-the-shelf, well-researched paper-and-pencil attitude instrument; of observations made during an ethnography of some employees' experiences; of the videotaping of verbal comments made during an interview; and so on.

In a more technical meaning, *reliability* refers to the strength of the shared systematic variance, usually conceptualized as some statistical association, between a theorized entity (e.g., a latent trait from a structural equation model) and an overt indicator of that theorized entity (e.g., scores resulting from a measurement process). Psychometricians often describe this shared variance (or association) through the theories of true and error scores, domain sampling, or "true scores and parallel tests" (Ghiselli, 1964, pp. 218-251; Ghiselli, Campbell, & Zedeck, 1981, pp. 195-222). Despite these formal, theoretical approaches to understanding reliability, similar conclusions are reached for definitional formulas and for their corresponding empirical estimates (e.g., user-friendly formulas). In other words, the more formal definitions and various theoretical approaches produce similar empirical estimates of reliability. For example, coefficient alpha usually assesses the internal consistency of scores, and test-retest coefficients usually assess the scores' stability over time. It is important to emphasize that the standard conceptualization of reliability (i.e., shared variance indexed by a statistical association) can be applied to scores obtained from, for example, numerically based standard paper-and-pencil tests, researchers' recorded interpretations made during intensive participant observer studies (i.e., field notes), or the verbal comments of interviewees. Note that each of these techniques constitutes a measurement process, and its outcomes can be taken as "scores."

Some level of confusion may occur when reliability is thought to apply to the measurement procedures themselves, rather than to the scored outcomes from these measurement procedures. Reliability does *not* apply to the data gathering methods themselves—to observations or interviews per se, or to standard paper-and-pencil job attitude instruments. Reliability *does* apply to the *properties of the scores' inferences*. Conceptually, then, it is quite appropriate to ask whether scores (e.g., interviewees' comments elicited by a researcher; observations recorded via field notes) from a qualitative study are consistent (e.g., repeatable under hypothetically identical or highly similar conditions) and stable (e.g., a researcher's interpretation of an employee's social construction of the firm's political situation remains relatively constant over time, presuming the situation itself also stays relatively constant). Whereas it would not be appropriate to conclude that a given survey instrument is reliable, it would be appropriate to conclude that the empirical estimates of reliability indicate reliable properties of the resulting scores.

When reliability is incorrectly attributed to measurement instruments, its conceptual meaning is often confused with its empirical estimate. That is, a researcher can mistakenly mix the definition of reliability with both a particular numeric value and the mechanical process that yielded that value. For example, a standard 8-item measure of job satisfaction might show high alpha-based internal consistency and high 2-week test-retest stability. These alpha and stability coefficients are sometimes taken to define reliability, rather than to be imperfect estimates for different properties of reliability. When taken as the definition, a specific reliability estimate may not, in fact, fit with a given qualitative study's method. It would be inappropriate, for instance, to argue that the over-time stability of behavioral observations made during a participant observer study can be established by an alpha-based formula for internal consistency. It would be appropriate, however, to ask whether these observations show some level of stability over time and to index that stability. Note that the concept of shared variance holds in this example; its empirical estimation does not.

Comment. It is important to reiterate that *reliability* refers to the shared systematic variance between a researcher's phenomenon of interest and its scored measurement. As one part of judging the quality of any study, the strength and nature of that conceptual association should be considered. I have suggested above that reliability is sometimes mistakenly interpreted as being interchangeable with its empirical estimates. As a result, it can *appear* that traditional notions of reliability do not apply to qualitative research. I would argue that reliability is a universally meaningful concept in the evaluation of both qualitative and quantitative organizational research.

Traditional Views on Validity

Whereas reliability is defined as the total amount of shared systematic variance, which includes any systematic error (or bias), validity is often defined as the shared "true" variance between an underlying concept and its empirical scores. In particular, true variance is defined to exclude systematic bias and to include only the "theoretically meaningful" systematic variance between an underlying idea and its overt representations. Thus, theory, some system of logic, or a clear specification for a focal concept is critical in determining what is and what is not true variance. Moreover, *true variance* can refer to a continuous relationship or a dichotomous association. In more exploratory, inductive studies, which seek to identify an underlying construct or process, validity remains a meaningful concept. The presence of validity would certainly be more difficult to infer and to document, however, because its theoretical basis would be less developed.

Based on the traditional psychometric definition, there is only one kind of validity. Accordingly, management researchers should strive to study true variance, both qualitatively and quantitatively. (These definitional relationships allow for the old—and correct—adages, "Reliability sets an upper bound to validity" and "Scores can be no more valid than their reliability.")

Although most formal presentations conclude that validity concerns explaining (or understanding) the shared true variance between an underlying concept and its manifest indicators, most descriptions imply various kinds of validity. Somewhat akin to mixing the conceptual definition of reliability with its empirical estimates, the implication of multiple kinds of validity reflects the erroneous mixing of a single conceptual definition—widely accepted as shared true variance—with its various empirical indices. Although it may appear to be only a semantic issue, there is substantial utility in defining one kind of validity that has multiple, though imperfect, forms. Whereas certain forms of validity may indeed not fit a given qualitative study's context or analytic situation, the larger concept of validity—shared true variance—holds merit for all management studies.

Below, the common forms of validity are summarized. Later in this chapter, I discuss how these common forms are typically conceptualized and applied by qualitative researchers.

Criterion-Related Validity

Evidence for criterion-related validity may be established if a statistical association is demonstrated between a predictor variable and some meaningful criterion. Most commonly, the statistical association is indexed by a Pearson product-moment correlation coefficient, but other statistics could be applied just as well (e.g., point-biserial correlation).

Two issues arise. First, it is *assumed* that the criterion itself is already reliably measured and meaningful. The criterion can be theoretically meaningful or deemed intrinsically valuable, as is often the case, for example, with job performance, accident rates, and absenteeism. Second, the predictor variable can be measured either before or simultaneous with the measurement of the criterion. If the predictor is measured before (at Time 1) the criterion (measured at Time 2), the design is called *predictive validity*. If the predictor and criterion are measured simultaneously, the design is called *concurrent validity*. Note that in order for comparable inferences to be drawn from predictive and concurrent validity designs, strong assumptions must be made that the effects of employees' natural maturation and job experience are unimportant or have already occurred. In sum, the inference of criterion-related validity is based on an empirical relationship.

Content Validity

Instead of the term *content validity*, some authors prefer to use the alternative label *content-oriented test construction*. As that name implies, evidence for this form of validity may be established if the procedures followed in constructing a measure (often called the test plan) are judged to derive "clearly and in a compelling fashion" from a meaningful conceptual domain. In contrast to the empirical orientation of criterion-related validity, the inference of content validity is based on the *qualitative judgment* that (a) the conceptual domain, (b) the test plan designed to map that conceptual domain, and (c) the resulting measurement instrument overlap substantially. Empirical data about reliability, item difficulty, and population norms can facilitate the judgment, but content validity is an essential qualitative judgment about content coverage.

Convergent and Discriminant Validity

Evidence for convergent validity may be established if scores from several measurement procedures that purport to measure the same (or very similar) concept are "highly" correlated. That is, scores from multiple measures of the same (or very similar) concept should converge. In contrast, evidence for discriminant validity may be established if scores from several measurement procedures that purport to measure different concepts are uncorrelated. Scores from multiple measures of different concepts should diverge. Scores from different measurement procedures for different concepts should diverge even more. In addition, there should be some indication that the convergent (or highly correlated) scores meaningfully differ from the divergent (or weakly correlated or uncorrelated) scores. Although exploratory or confirmatory factor analysis can clarify matters, it is ultimately a matter of qualitative judgment as to what constitute sufficient convergence and sufficient divergence.

Construct Validity

In perhaps its most abstract form, construct validity is a continuous, ongoing process of accumulating evidence that suggests scores from a measurement procedure reflect its intended construct. In other words, do scores actually measure what a researcher claims they do, and not something else? As such, construct validity subsumes all the forms of validity discussed above, and the argument can more readily be made that there is only one kind of validity, albeit with many forms.

Although a continuous, ongoing process of accumulating evidence, construct validity can be established only through the presentation of a substantial body of data. Nonetheless, when "sufficient evidence" has been accumulated remains a subjective judgment. Some recent examples are illustrative. Mowday, Steers, and Porter (1979) define the conceptual domain for their construct of interest, organizational commitment, and carefully describe the procedures they used in constructing their measurement instrument. They then present data from nine samples of employees that support judgments for internal consistency, test-retest reliability, convergent validity, discriminant validity, and predictive validity. In similar fashion, Pierce, Gardner, Cummings, and Dunham (1989) define the conceptual domain for their construct of interest, organization-based self-esteem, and carefully describe their test construction procedures. They then present data from seven studies and empirical evidence that supports judgments for internal consistency, stability over time, convergent validity, discriminant validity, incremental validity, predictive validity, and concurrent validity.

In a somewhat different fashion, Van Dyne, Graham, and Dienesch (1994) attempt to redefine, measure, and validate their construct of interest, organizational citizenship behavior. These researchers carefully describe their construct domain, measurement procedures, and theory-based hypotheses about the construct's "nomological network" (a set of theoretically relevant variables). Across six independent data sets, they report evidence suggesting internal consistency, test-retest reliability, and the empirical relationships between organizational citizenship behavior and the set of theoretically relevant variables.

Across these three examples, it should be noted that the central issue is not whether construct validity was demonstrated. Rather, the key issue is the qualitative judgment that sufficient evidence has been gathered for construct validity to be demonstrated.

Generalizability and
Other Forms of Validity

Primarily from experimentally oriented research, *internal validity* refers to the judgment that an experiment's procedures are sufficient to justify rejection or provisional acceptance of its hypotheses. For example, if an experiment's focus is on work effort, does the experimental task in fact reflect the effects of effort, and not some alternative factor (e.g., prior experience)?

External validity refers to the judgment that an experiment's results can be generalized to a larger population or to an alternative population. For instance, does the experiment's random sampling of college students allow generalization of the study's results to the larger U.S. workforce?

Although less often seen, *ecological validity* refers to the judgment that a study's or an experiment's features include or reflect the major features of the context in which the phenomenon of interest is found. Whereas the absence of these features implies ecological invalidity, their presence implies ecological validity. For example, if interest centers on when a firm decides to sell a new retail product, does the study's design features include the major contextual characteristics that surround those decisions (e.g., Staw, Barsade, & Koput, 1997)? Because of its heavy emphasis on context, as well as its judged importance, ecological validity is particularly important to the evaluation of most qualitative research.

Comment

It cannot be overemphasized that *validity* refers to the shared true variance between a researcher's phenomenon of interest and its scored measurement. As another part of judging the quality of any study, the strength and nature of that conceptual association should be considered. Akin to reliability, validity is sometimes mistakenly taken to be interchangeable with one (or more) of its forms. As a result, it only appears that traditional views on validity do not apply to qualitative research. Again, I would argue that the concept of validity is universally meaningful to the evaluation of both qualitative and quantitative organizational research.

As suggested above, there are numerous empirical estimates of reliability and validity. Although heavily influenced by these empirical estimates, as well as accompanying rhetorical arguments, decisions about reliability and validity ultimately rest upon the researchers' and readers' judgment about sufficient or systematic true variance between an underlying notion and its objective indicators. At issue is whether or not these judgments and the circumstances in which they occur (i.e., their real or simulated organizational contexts) legitimately hold for qualitative studies. I would argue that they do. This question is addressed more directly below; moreover, the interrelatedness of these various forms of validity is a recurring theme in the next section.

Conceptualization and Measurement in Qualitative Research

I should note again that the qualitative methodologists whose work is discussed in this section are not known as organizational researchers. Thus, their viewpoints derive from research, standards, and norms in other social sciences. Nonetheless, their collective views are instructive and may be useful for drawing conclusions about and developing recommendations for organizational science. The following subsections address the work of Yin (1994) and Kvale (1996), who refer to the reliability and validity of specific qualitative methods, and the work of

Marshall and Rossman (1995) and Maxwell (1996), who discuss reliability and validity in qualitative research in general.

As I have mentioned, the topics of reliability and validity are somewhat controversial among qualitative researchers. Kvale (1996) notes that some qualitative researchers ignore or dismiss these ideas as oppressive, inconsequential, or irrelevant remnants of outdated positivist philosophies of science. Other qualitative researchers adopt a more moderate position and advise addressing these issues directly (e.g., Lincoln & Guba, 1985; Marshall & Rossman, 1995; Maxwell, 1996; Yin, 1994). Like these more moderate writers, I hold that the traditional (and still cardinal) concepts of reliability and validity are socially constructed, pluralistic, and compatible with multiple and coexisting worldviews. In addition, I assume that there is at least some level of agreement among people on the systematic regularity within any organizational context or contexts (Roberts, Hulin, & Rousseau, 1978).

Yin's Case Study Research

Yin (1994, pp. 32-38) argues that four standards (or "tests," in his terms) are commonly applied in the establishment of the quality of any social scientific study. Thus, these standards are relevant to case study and other forms of qualitative research as well. These four tests are (a) construct validity, which is to establish correct "operational measures for the concepts being studied"; (b) internal validity, which is to establish, "for explanatory or causal studies only, and not for descriptive or exploratory studies . . . a causal relationship, whereby certain conditions are shown to lead to other conditions, as distinguished from spurious relationships"; (c) external validity, which is to establish "the domain to which a study's findings can be generalized"; and (d) reliability, which is to demonstrate "that the operations of a study—such as the data collection procedures—can be repeated, with the same results."

Construct validity. In order to establish that "a measurement actually measures what the research claims it does and not something else," Yin recommends three specific tactics. First, multiple sources of evidence can be accessed in order to capitalize on a source's unique strengths and to compensate for its weaknesses. In particular, Yin suggests that researchers undertake one or preferably more of the following: (a) Examine documents, such as letters, formal reports, newspaper articles, and participants' personal notes; (b) search archival records, such as official company records, government census and sample data, and older commercially available data sets; (c) interview people; (d) observe the case's setting; (e) participate in the case's setting; and (f) examine physical artifacts. Second, the researcher might establish a "chain of evidence." That is, the obtained data should result from a sequential (measurement) process that follows (or shows) a clear and compelling logic (e.g., a preliminary or developed theory). The reader of a case study research report should be able to reconstruct and anticipate the sequential logic. The clearer and more compelling the logic, the stronger the argument for construct validity. Third, key informants (e.g., interviewees) should review the case study report to ensure its veracity, honesty, and clarity. With feedback from informants, a qualitative researcher is less likely to impose incorrect interpretations (or worldviews) accidentally based on his or her own perspective on the study's data.

Comment. Yin's recommended tactics bear a striking similarity to the traditional notions of convergent, discriminant, and construct validity. In particular, multiple sources of information should converge and diverge as predicted by theory or some evolving logic—the conventional notions of convergent and discriminant validity. A "chain of evidence" implies ongoing efforts to establish a nomological network, which is the common idea for construct validity. The use of multiple informants implies internal consistency and potentially stability over time, which appears to be the traditional notion of reliability.

Internal validity. In order to reduce the potential for alternative explanations to a researcher's claim of causation, Yin recommends three related tactics. First, pattern matching might be conducted. For instance, the researcher generates a series of theoretically or conceptually relevant predictions and then collects empirical data to test those predictions. Evidence of internal validity can be inferred from the pattern of agreement between predicted and empirical outcomes. Yin's second tactic is explanation building. For example, the researcher states an initial theory or set of propositions and then examines the findings from an initial case for its consistency with the theory or propositions. Depending upon the judged fit, the researcher then modifies the initial theory or propositions.

Sequentially, the researcher examines additional cases, judges them for fit, and makes modifications. Through this iterative process, evidence for internal validity becomes enhanced. Third, time series designs may be adopted; these are akin to time series designs from experimental research. For many causally connected events, a specific time-based sequence can be predicted. A researcher can examine case study data to verify the predicted time sequence and then infer evidence for internal validity to the extent that the time sequence is found to hold.

Comment. Yin's notion of internal validity bears a striking resemblance to the empirically driven and traditional notions of criterion-related validity and reliability. That is, pattern matching appears to ask whether scores objectively connect to (or predict) some expected criterion or criteria, which is the conventional idea for criterion-related validity. Explanation building appears to ask whether scores derive from some internally consistent logic, and time series designs appear to ask about stability over time. Both of these tactics address the traditional notion of reliability.

External validity. In order to document the generalizability of findings from a particular case study, Yin recommends a single tactic: The case must be replicated in another situation. Thus, a second (or more) independent case (or cases) must be conducted. Depending upon the researcher's theory, the alternative situation might be quite similar to or different from the original case study. The decision about how similar (or different) depends heavily on the researcher's application of "analytic generalizability," which case study research in particular, and much of qualitative research in general, often evokes.

Comment. In Yin's application, *analytic generalizability* refers to the extent an existing theory can serve as a template for evaluating the results of a case study. If two or more cases show similar results, the underlying theory receives corroboration, with the second case providing evidence of external validity. It is important to highlight that case study research does *not* involve probabilistically based sampling. Thus, statistical generalization to a larger population, or statistical inference, should not and cannot be evoked. Instead, case study research has a more deterministic flavor. That is, the theoretical proposition, concept, construct, or idea *fits, partially fits,* or *does not fit* with the facts of the case under study. Following a widely accepted academic value, the logic of replication holds for both quantitative and qualitative research. By inference, the traditional concept of validity appears again to be universally meaningful in organizational research.

Reliability. To determine whether a case study's procedures can be repeated, Yin recommends two tactics. First, the researcher should write a thorough case protocol. Yin considers the protocol to be more than a simple research tool; it is the set of specific procedures and general principles laid out for the study by the researcher. At a minimum, it should specify (a) an overview of the case study's objectives and research issues, (b) field procedures (e.g., researcher credentials, site specifications, sources of information), (c) case study questions (e.g., the specific research questions under study, interview schedules and topics, and method of data analysis), and (d) the structure of the case study report. Second, the researcher should create the case study's database. Whether the physical data consist of field notes from participant observations, audiotaped or transcribed interviews, or archival records, they should be arrayed in a manner that lends itself to external inspection and reanalysis. Through detailed specification and data documentation, inferences about the *repeatability* of the specific case study increase. In this fourth quality standard, Yin directly applies the traditional notion of reliability.

Summary. Many traditional elements of the concepts of reliability and validity are found in Yin's notions about qualitative research in general and case studies in particular. Although specific tactics (or empirical indicators) certainly differ between quantitative and qualitative studies, the cardinal ideas of reliability and validity remain meaningful for the evaluation of all organizational research.

Kvale on Generalizability and Reliability

Kvale (1996) summarizes the main elements of qualitative research as follows: (a) a substantial amount of time spent by the researcher on site; (b) intensive researcher contact with the site's participants, operations, and activities; and (c) an active, dynamic effort on the part of the researcher to understand these participants, operations, and activities in their natural contexts. Thus, generalization from qualitative research is often questioned, but it can be addressed through the following three judgments.

Naturalistic generalization. With naturalistic generalization, judgment about the generalizability of a qualitative study's results to another context is based on the researcher's personal experience. In particular, this judgment derives from the researcher's tacit knowledge about participants, operations, and activities, and how they affect one another. Almost certainly, most persons would acknowledge that at least some meaningful generalization can occur naturally. Nonetheless, naturalistic generalization would likely be a difficult argument to make in a compelling fashion to many organizational researchers. Too often, for instance, qualitative management researchers rely on (a) access to a case's participants, operations, and activities, and (b) rhetorical devices such as selected quotes to document a study's generalizability (Larsson & Lowendahl, 1996). In other words, they say, "Trust us."

Comment. Such appeals are weak and insufficient. Unless they can make a compelling case, qualitative researchers in management might be better advised to avoid arguing for naturalistic generalizability and to apply their arguments directly in favor of analytic generalizability (described below and by Yin, 1994).

Statistical generalization. To the vast majority of organizational researchers, statistical generalization is a much more familiar idea than naturalistic generalization. It is based on formal notions of random sampling, estimating parameters, and derivation of standard errors. Because few qualitative studies draw random samples, the applicability of statistical generalization to qualitative research is limited. Accordingly, few qualitative researchers apply this argument.

Analytic generalization. In analytic generalization, a "reasoned judgment" is made about whether the results from one qualitative study, along with its particular context, can legitimately guide inferences for another study, along with its particular context. At its core, a judgment for or against analytic generalizability is based on an analysis of the similarities and differences between the contexts of two studies. More specifically, the major and salient features of one study's context are compared with and argued to be sufficiently similar to those of another context. The more compelling the arguments, the stronger the inference for analytic generalizability. Kvale suggests that these arguments should be grounded in case-law-like logic, which can serve as a useful prototype for this core judgment. As in any research, in qualitative research judgments about analytic generalization are the responsibility of both the researcher and the reader of the research report. Thus, management researchers should offer very direct reasons in favor of analytic generalizability. For example, the qualitative researcher might present a point-by-point comparison of similarities and differences between contrasted contexts. In more traditional terms, analytic generalizability is akin to ecological validity. In my opinion, however, the term *analytic generalizability* implies much more depth than does the term *ecological validity*.

Reliability. Kvale follows the traditional notion of reliability, which pertains to the consistency of research results. Unreliability is often due, for instance, to misleading questions, inaccurate transcriptions of recorded speech, or faulty categorization decisions by researchers.

Summary. Kvale recommends that qualitative researchers directly address the issues of external validity, ecological validity, and reliability. His notions about analytic generalization strongly resemble the traditional concept of ecological validity. Moreover, his notions about reliability appear quite mainstream.

Kvale on Validity in a Postmodern World

The modern world. Many qualitative researchers equate the "modern world" with the natural (and sometimes the more limited physical) science model. That is, there is an objective world and there are objective truths, and traditional positivist notions of science should lead to the discovery and understanding of those truths. In this modern world, scientific validity can be best understood through the assessment of the truthfulness of its statements using three traditional positivist criteria for truth. First, the *correspondence* criterion involves the accuracy (or strength of relationships) between the scientific statements and the objective world. Specifically, do objective data from the empirical world fit with these statements? Second, the *coherence* criterion concerns the internal logic or consistency among scientific statements. In other words, do the statements follow a clear system of thinking? Third, the *pragmatic* criterion involves the practical outcomes of the scientific statements. Do predictable (and managerially relevant) consequences occur from the application of these truth statements?

The postmodern world. Along these lines, many qualitative researchers define the "postmodern world" (or simply the postmodern) as the rejection of the natural (or physical) science model. Instead, empirical reality is seen as a social entity, and truth is therefore socially constructed (for example, through dialogue). Thus, there are many possible world-views, truths, and criteria for truth. In these socially constructed worlds, the traditional criteria for truth are not necessarily wrong, but they may be more or less correct, depending upon one's point of view. Because of the assumed pluralistic nature of truth, postmodern approaches to validity center on falsification of competing worldviews. In particular, Kvale identifies three forms of validity (or falsification): validity as craftsmanship, validity as communication, and pragmatic validity.

Validity as craftsmanship. Although not limited to a postmodern view, validity as craftsmanship encompasses a study's methods and theory as well as the researcher's character, integrity, and scholarly record. More specifically, validity as craftsmanship involves the trustworthiness of a study's results, and it is most directly conceptualized by the strength of a study's falsification attempts. The stronger the attempt, the greater can be the inference for validity as craftsmanship.

Kvale highlights three particular tactics that enhance judgments about validity as craftsmanship. First, the researcher must adopt a critical outlook during the analysis. He or she should openly state personal biases and include checks (or controls) for selective perceptions and biased interpretations. For example, it is often desirable to designate a member of the research team to play devil's advocate during the planning and data collection phases of a study. Second, the purpose and content of the study must precede its method. Although unfortunate, one often hears stories about qualitative researchers who expend considerable time, effort, and money collecting substantial amounts of data only to be at a loss as to what to do next. In such circumstances, most qualitative researchers would likely recommend starting over. Third, the research must be tightly connected to theory creation or testing. Those studies that are more inductive and oriented toward theory creation can be judged by how well the data lead to testable propositions. Moreover, these inductive studies can also be evaluated according to the strength of their preliminary tests of those, albeit tentative, propositions. Studies that are more deductive and oriented toward theory testing can be judged directly by the strength of their falsification efforts.

Comment. Although somewhat broader in scope, validity as craftsmanship appears akin to the traditional notion of internal validity. In the aggregate, both concepts appear to focus on the trustworthiness of a study's purported causal effects. Moreover, they also focus on the anticipation and elimination of alternative explanations.

Validity as communication. Originating in language-based disciplines (e.g., rhetoric, comparative literature), validity as communication demonstrates hermeneutic traditions, or the study of how (usually print-based) texts are interpreted. Its two basic theses are that truth can be tested through dialogue and that validity as communication can be inferred from the quality of argument between conflicting claims.

Thus, three issues most directly determine the judgment of validity of communication. First, communication and truth testing involve persuasion through rational discourse. Most important, it is the quality of this discourse that directly determines validity as communication. Simply put, the more persuasive the argument, the stronger the position's inferred validity. Such discourse may occur in the U.S. legal system, in formal debates at the national meetings of the Academy of Management, or in conflicting streams of journal articles about the superiority of competing theories.

Second, the criteria or purpose of the discourse should be clear. Often in academic and scientific debates, consensus (sometimes referred to as consensual validation) is the ultimate goal (e.g., Kuhn, 1996). A theory is judged valid when the preponderance of practitioners, researchers, and more neutral observers in a discipline come to accept it as correct, strongest, or generally valid. Furthermore, the higher this preponderance, the stronger the inference for validity as communication.

Third, the interests of the debating parties should be made clear as well. For example, confidence in a theorist's arguments, corroborating data, and applied methods might be lessened if that individual is the theory's sole advocate. In contrast, confidence in similar arguments, data, and methods might be enhanced if the advocate is seen as more neutral. The more detached the debating party, the stronger the inference for validity as communication.

Comment. Although based on traditions quite distant from organizational science, validity as communication involves the strength, persuasiveness, and modes of presentation of theory (or a construct or idea). Furthermore, it appears to rely, at least in part, on the interconnectedness between rhetorical arguments and any empirical data that bolster those arguments. As such, validity as communication appears akin to the traditional notions of content and construct validity.

Pragmatic validity. Beyond an argument's persuasiveness, pragmatic validity involves the real-world changes that occur as a result of a researcher's theory, propositions, or actions. It can include traditional notions of criterion-related validity, but a broader and perhaps deeper effect is meant. Inferences of pragmatic validity can be made at two levels. First, a theory, proposition, or action can induce verbal changes. For instance, an argument's persuasiveness may elicit verbal agreement with that argument on a subsequent interview question or survey item. Second, a theory, proposition, or action can induce behavioral changes as well. For many years, quantitative research reports from numerous disciplines routinely reported tests of statistical significance. At the same time, it was debated whether effect sizes should routinely accompany these reported tests of statistical significance. The arguments in favor of reporting effect sizes quickly won the verbal favor of researchers (level 1), but it took many more years before many of these same researchers actually began reporting their statistical effect sizes (level 2). Thus, pragmatic validity can be inferred from the verbal statements agreeing to the practice. However, even more pragmatic validity can be inferred from the behavioral changes. In the aggregate, and to reiterate an earlier point, pragmatic validity not only includes the traditional notion of criterion-related validity, but it would appear to impose even stronger empirical requirements.

Comment

In Kvale's view, validity in qualitative research involves debate, belief, and action. Although the overt signs of validity may vary across studies, qualitative and quantitative research appear to have more similarities than differences. In particular, both traditions encourage researchers to anticipate and eliminate potential problems before they occur. Furthermore, both traditions encourage researchers to respond to problems after they occur through efforts aimed at discounting the significance of those problems. Whether qualitative and quantitative researchers practice more or less a proactive or reactive model varies by individual study.

Marshall and Rossman's "Criteria for Soundness"

Marshall and Rossman (1995, pp. 143-145) assert that the quality of qualitative research can be determined through the evaluation of four characteristics: credibility, transferability, replicability, and confirmability.

Credibility. A qualitative study's credibility is related to the accuracy and completeness with which the phenomenon of interest—which can be a construct, a theoretical process, or a hypothetical entity—is identified and described. In particular, accuracy and completeness of the phenomenon's description should be determined from the participant's—as opposed to the researcher's—point of view. For example, has the participant's cause map, cognitive schema, or worldview been successfully captured by the researcher? The fuller this description, the stronger the inference for the study's credibility. Thus, rich description of the phenomenon itself—its setting, its meaningful participants, and its dynamic characteristics—is essential for a study's validity.

Comment. In more traditional terms, credibility implies that the qualitative researcher must address, in part, the general issue of internal validity. That is, the researcher must render judgments about (a) whether internal processes occurred as described; (b) whether the purported causal agents, social mechanisms, and psychological processes operated as predicted; and (c) whether these processes, agents, and mechanisms are as interconnected as expected based on existing or evolving theory.

Transferability. A qualitative study's transferability is related to the generalizability of the study's inferences. At least two judgments are involved. At one level, the researcher must make a judgment about the generalizability of the study's results to the larger but same population. This first judgment is akin to the traditional statistical sampling notion of generalizability. Because qualitative research does not commonly draw random or convenience samples, which serve as surrogates for random samples, this first judgment is usually far from precise. Nonetheless, it must be based on an overall assessment of whether the study's features (i.e., it's credibility; e.g., rich descriptions of the phenomenon's context) are sufficient to allow generalizing to similar types of people and settings. The greater the judged similarity, the stronger the inference for a study's transferability. In more traditional terms, the qualitative researcher must address the issue of external validity.

At a second level, the researcher must also make a judgment about the generalizability of the study's results to other populations and settings. Whereas the first judgment is often based on the study's features (i.e., its credibility), this second judgment is based on the assessed strength of the underlying theoretical arguments. In more deductive, theory-testing studies, this second-level generalizing can readily occur. In more inductive, theory-generating studies, however, this second-level generalizing becomes more difficult, because, in part, the study's underlying theory (or construct or idea) is still evolving. In more traditional terms, the qualitative researcher must address the issue of ecological validity. Moreover, it should be noted that qualitative researchers often place a premium on a study's ecological validity, far more so than many quantitative researchers and a great deal more so than those who tend toward laboratory-based experimental designs.

Confirmability. In qualitative research, confirmability is related to a study's objectivity. That is, could a study's findings be confirmed by independent persons? At some point, the researcher must anticipate, eliminate, minimize, or discount his or her own biases. In more traditional terms, the qualitative researcher must address the issues of reliability, where unsystematic error is eliminated, and construct validity, where systematic error (or bias) is eliminated.

Replicability. In qualitative research, replicability is related to dependability. More specifically, it means that the researcher should account for (or explain) the dynamic, changing qualities of the study's phenomenon of interest. One of the many potential strengths of qualitative research is its detailed emphasis on and flexibility toward changes over time. When the focal construct, process, or entity is dynamic, the qualitative study must have some mechanism to assess these changes. In more traditional terms, it has been argued that the qualitative researcher must address the issue of reliability (Lincoln & Guba, 1985).

Marshall and Rossman argue that the emphasis on changes over time renders traditional notions of reliability nonapplicable to qualitative research. They argue that classic reliability theory, grounded in quantitative traditions, assumes an unchanging world that readily lends itself to assessment of a study's replicability. Under conditions assumed by traditional reliability theory, estimates of consistency and stability can be reasonably made. Because most qualitative researchers deal with a social world that is interpretative and under constant social construction, static notions about the phenomena of interest, which are implied to mean traditional notions about reliability and replicability, should not and cannot apply.

Although Marshall and Rossman offer substantial insight into an understanding of qualitative research, I disagree with their opinion on the meaningfulness of reliability. Certainly, specific empirical estimates for internal consistency or stability may indeed not effectively apply to dynamic processes. However, the notion of reliability itself—the shared systematic variance between some concept and its manifest indicator, which can be a researcher's observation—applies equally well to dynamic and static concepts. To the extent that individuals are continually constructing their social worlds, reliability must also involve any constancy in how they so construct those worlds. In other words, high reliability implies more systematic construction over time (given hypothetically similar contexts), and low reliability implies less systematic construction over time (given hypothetically similar contexts). Correspondingly, a reasonable index of that constancy would need to account for that systematic change over time.

Specific tactics. Marshall and Rossman suggest that establishing their four criteria for soundness can be facilitated by several actions. First, someone on the research team or outside the research team should be assigned to play the role of devil's advocate. This person would serve to maintain the critical questioning of the study's quality and the researchers' assumptions. Second, all people associated with the research should engage in a constant search for negative (or theory-negating) incidents. A focus on disconfirmation serves to lessen potential biases. Third, constant checking for the plausibility of rival hypotheses should be conducted. This serves also to maintain the critical questioning of the study's quality and researchers' assumptions. Fourth, the researchers should practice value-free note taking. Such note taking does not occur naturally or easily; it is a learned skill. Fifth, checks on the accuracy of data collection and veracity of the methods for data analysis should be designed into the study and periodically conducted.

Comment. These tactics, singularly or collectively, have great merit. They should be routinely considered and, when feasible, applied to all management studies. Their application can only enhance confidence in a qualitative study.

Maxwell on Threats to Validity

Maxwell (1996, pp. 86-98) argues that validity is the "key issue" in qualitative research design. In particular, validity is a goal and not a product of a particular method. It is inferred based on accumulated evidence and the relationship between a study and its purpose. In other words, do the researcher's inferences follow from the study's data and particular context? At an operational level, the inference of validity in qualitative research derives from the evidence that discounts alternative explanations of the researcher's inferences. The more alternatives that can be eliminated as implausibility, the stronger the inference for validity. Furthermore, Maxwell discusses three "kinds" of validity: description, interpretation, and theory.

Description. Valid description is related to the accuracy with which what the researcher saw, heard, and experienced is represented in the data. To minimize the threat of inaccuracy, Maxwell recommends that researchers employ audiotape, videotape, and verbatim transcriptions of text. Lack of financial resources, faulty equipment, poor familiarity with the equipment, and sloppy typing can, for example, seriously restrict valid description. In more traditional terms, valid description appears to be related to reliability. That is, are the data reproducible, presumably for subsequent analyses?

Interpretation. Valid interpretation is the correspondence between what the study's participants meant and what the researcher inferred. That is, did the researcher learn the participants' intended meaning, or did he or she impose an alternative perspective (or meaning)? Maxwell suggests that poor interpretation validity can result from the use of leading questions, too-brief responses, and the researcher's lack of attention. To minimize the threat of poor understanding, the researcher can seek "member checks." For example, the study's participants might provide a subsequent evaluation of the researcher's interpretation of the data. In more traditional terms, valid interpretation appears to be related to construct validity. That is, do the researcher's inferences actually mean what they are purported to mean?

Theory. Valid theory is related to the researcher's efforts aimed at discounting alternative explanations for the study findings. Maxwell suggests that the most common and serious threat to valid theory is simply the researcher's ignoring discrepant data. Personal biases, pet theories, and strong a priori convictions can blind researchers to the existence or meaning of potentially disconfirming findings. In more traditional terms, valid theory appears to be related to construct validity.

Maxwell's Specific Tactics

Maxwell (1996) suggests that most serious threats to validity come from the personal biases of the researcher and the participants' reactions to the study (i.e., organizational behaviors are affected by the research process itself; e.g., people act differently in the presence of a participant observer than they would otherwise). He recommends eight tactics to minimize these (and other) threats.

First, the researcher should identify and empirically test with data as many alternative explanations as possible. Because all plausible alternatives cannot be identified, let alone tested with data, Maxwell notes that this approach cannot be reduced to a formula—a researcher's skill and insight are required. Second, the researcher must make a proactive effort to identify discrepant and negative cases. The examination of potentially invalidating data appears to mirror the widely accepted idea that rigorous attempts to refute ideas define good science. Third, the researcher should employ triangulating methods, which will serve to minimize particular biases. Because no method is bias-free, corroboration with multiple methods implies negation of many biases. In other words, results should converge across multiple methods. Fourth, the researcher should give the study's participants a chance to react to the study's data and conclusions. Because participants' worldviews are of focal interest, directly asking for their corroboration serves as a strong check on the effects of the researcher's personal biases. Fifth, the researcher should attempt to collect comprehensive and descriptively rich data, which will also lessen the likelihood of significant omissions. Sixth, the researcher should "count the countable" (see Chapter 6). That is, where feasible and theoretically meaningful, quantitative analyses might be applied. Seventh, the researcher should seek feedback from an external and neutral third party, as this can keep the research "honest." Finally, the researcher should compare the research, cases, or data to other research, cases, or data to enhance confidence in converging empirical results.

Comment. To a large extent, Maxwell appears to be describing the traditional notion of construct validity. If the phrase *researcher's inferences* implies the outcome of "some measurement process," these inferences constitute scores. If the term *follow* implies fit of these scores within some nomological network (or logic or theory), traditional notions of construct validity are being described. If the phrases *eliminated as implausible* and *accumulated evidence* imply an ongoing process, judgments about the strength of construct validity are strongly suggested.

Conclusion

Both qualitative and quantitative researchers look for and evaluate various signs of their studies' soundness. Nonetheless, there is a mistaken idea among many management scholars that these signs are fundamentally different for both groups. The focus of this chapter has been that these signs are in fact very similar. It is sometimes said, for example, that quantitative researchers adopt a proactive view, whereas qualitative researchers adopt a reactive view. More specifically, the former attempt to control for error statistically or experimentally, whereas the latter attempt to account for or explain away error. In fact, all organizational studies involve proactive and reactive concerns about error. Both camps endeavor to anticipate problems and eliminate them before they occur, and both try to identify problems before, during, and after data collection and to discount their significance.

A few qualitative researchers hold that social construction of organizational life is so pervasive that agreement among participants is negligible. As a result, consistency, stability, and shared systematic variance between an idea and its manifest observations are so inherently slight that traditional notions about reliability and validity, though nice ideas, do not hold value for their research. The world changes too quickly, it is too subjective, and everyone socially constructs differently. This extreme position is somewhat comparable to that of those few quantitative researchers in management who dogmatically hold that the vast preponderance of laboratory research is irrelevant and that only field studies are meaningful.

Under such an extreme view, discussion about reliability and validity in qualitative research may indeed seem pointless. Moreover, those qualitative researchers who hold such an extreme view would appear constrained to describe individual circumstances and precluded from the traditional scientific goal of accumulating knowledge. From a certain point of view, these researchers would also seem precluded from "doing organizational science." That is, they appear restricted to journalistic accounts of organizational life. Though potentially insightful, their work would not be science as defined by the larger managerial discipline, common definitions of science, or standard practice.

Finally, it should be acknowledged that determinations about reliability and validity are inherently judgmental. Moreover, what signs are judged may appear to differ between qualitative and quantitative studies, but their basic content is the same. Researchers' judgments are not restricted to qualitative studies and precluded from quantitative research. Any study's conceptualizations, measurement processes, and interpretations should be judged as carefully made, systematically addressed, and representative of the study's intended underlying construct (or idea or theory).

Ultimately, the burden falls on the organizational researcher to present a compelling case for the reliability and validity within his or her study. In particular, the researcher should design into the research project as many checks and tactics as practically feasible. Moreover, it is imperative that some discussion of the results of these checks be included in any qualitative research report. In the absence of such text, discourse, or discussion, such a research report may not merit journal space. In the next chapter, I offer some recommendations regarding the content of any manuscript that reports a qualitative study and is submitted to a management journal.

Conclusions

This final chapter recaps and reiterates the main themes of the preceding chapters. Also, specific recommendations are offered concerning what a reader and reviewer should readily learn from a manuscript that describes a qualitative study and is submitted to a management journal. These recommendations are offered as a series of 42 questions. If a reviewer cannot answer all of these questions after a single reading, the manuscript may need revision; if the reviewer can answer few of the questions, the manuscript may merit rejection.

Reiteration of Themes

As this volume draws toward its end, it may be useful to recap the themes of the preceding chapters. Reflecting my advice throughout this book on how to conduct qualitative research, Chapter 1 presents my biases, goals, and worldview on how and why qualitative research has been practiced in organizational science (i.e., the "tensions" and the "middle ground"). In a nutshell, I assert that qualitative research methods have been underutilized by organizational researchers. However, the current topics under study by organizational scientists are now prompting many scholars to take a more careful look at these alternative, qualitative tools and techniques. I also strongly advocate that qualitative methods be *blended* with the quantitative methods in use in mainstream organizational science.

In Chapter 2, the main question addressed is, What are the major domains and components of qualitative research? In my judgment, the main domains have been best articulated by Miles and Huberman (1994), who describe them as (a) participant observer, (b) nonparticipant observer, (c) interviewing, and (d) archival studies. Across these domains and other taxonomies as well, four underlying themes are identified: that qualitative research (a) occurs in natural settings, (b) derives from the participants' perspective, (c) is flexible, and (d) has few standardized methods or procedures (see Table 2.1). In addition, substantial disagreement exists on what constitutes the main components of qualitative research. Nevertheless, two underlying themes can be identified across several taxonomic systems: that the components of qualitative research should serve to *reduce* the amount of data while simultaneously *enhancing* the data's meaning (see Table 2.2).

In Chapter 3, the main questions are (a) How does one begin qualitative research? and (b) What specific designs might one adopt? With respect to the former question, it all begins with the judgment that qualitative methods are best suited to the research question or analytic situation at hand. As summarized in Table 3.1, qualitative research is well suited to issues of description, interpretation, and explanation, but it is not well suited to the investigation of issues of prevalence, generalizability, or calibration. With respect to the latter question, the use of grounded theory or focus groups is recommended when research interest focuses on the *generation* of theory, whereas the use of case studies or conversational interviews is recommended when research interest focuses on the *testing* (or falsification) of theory.

Chapters 4 and 5 move to the issue of specific techniques and tactics in qualitative research. Their primary and collective question is, What does one actually do when conducting qualitative research? As such, details in the application of numerous techniques and tactics are provided throughout these two chapters. Because of this detail, however, a major issue in qualitative research methods can be easily overlooked. That is, a single technique is rarely applied in a single study. More commonly, multiple tactics are necessary. Thus, the qualitative researcher is advised to think carefully about creating hybrid techniques or combining techniques within a single study.

In Chapter 6, the point is made that quantitative data are routinely collected in most qualitative studies (e.g., two-phase design). Often, these data are categorical in nature and are not as effectively analyzed as they might be. Thus, Chapter 6 asks the question, Which methods of categorical data analysis are likely to be useful in the quantitative analysis of qualitative data? In response, four indices of association, five types of correlations, and two forms of generalized linear models are offered.

Finally, Chapter 7 turns to perhaps the most important issue in this book: How does one judge the quality of qualitative research? The answer is reflected in the chapter's title, "The Cardinal Concepts of Reliability and Validity." Throughout Chapter 7, it is demonstrated that these universal standards for evaluation are applicable to both qualitative and quantitative research.

The Research Report

In addition to conducting empirical research, the scientific mission of organizational researchers requires that they share their findings. As it is for many academic disciplines, the primary mechanism for the sharing of research is the scholarly journal article. Although the peer review process is imperfect (and seems particularly so after one receives a rejection letter), the norms in organizational science dictate that manuscript submissions for potential journal publication must be subjected to this process, which has become the field's main quality control mechanism. Thus, it would benefit the profession, the research, and individual researchers if some agreement could be reached on what should appear in qualitative research reports.

Although there are no hard-and-fast rules about what must necessarily enter into a qualitative study, the norms in organizational science and the mores of the various disciplines that commonly practice qualitative research allow for some suggested guidelines as to what *should* be included in a manuscript submitted to a management journal. Below, I offer some specific recommendations about what readers and reviewers should *readily* learn from a submitted manuscript. The recommendations are offered as a series of 42 questions. Readers and reviewers should be able to answer most, if not all, of these questions after a single reading of a potential (e.g., before it is sent for colleagues' comments) or actual (e.g., the revision based on these colleagues' comments) journal submission. If some answers are not readily apparent, the manuscript likely requires revision. If too few of the questions can be answered, the manuscript may merit rejection. (For other sets of relevant recommendations, see Campion, 1993; Kvale, 1996.)

Theoretical or Conceptual Basis

1. Was the study derived from a (a) formal theory, (b) semideveloped conceptual structure, or (c) general topic?
2. Did the study serve to (a) generate new theory, (b) extend or elaborate existing theory, or (c) not generate new theory?
3. Is the study's theory or general topic sufficiently interesting to merit journal pages?

Because the organizational sciences have a strong applied tradition, a practical application, instead of a theoretical basis, can also justify a study.

4. Did the researcher intend to solve a distinct managerial problem or concern?
5. Is the study's problem or concern sufficiently important to merit journal pages?

Literature Review

6. Are key references cited?
7. Are "critical" references cited?
8. Are too many references cited, such that they distract more than they clarify?
9. Are the references accurate?

Conceptual Development

The following questions presume theory testing and the appropriateness of hypothesis testing. If these presumptions are incorrect, these questions should be ignored.

10. Are hypotheses presented at the appropriate level of analysis?
11. Are the hypotheses falsifiable?
12. Are the hypotheses central to their theoretical, conceptual, or applied basis?
13. Do the hypotheses involve theorized processes or outcomes?
14. Are the hypotheses adequately operationalized?
15. Do the hypotheses derive from "key" or "central" constructs (e.g., persons, events, places)?

Sample and Context

16. Was subject selection based on (a) random sampling, (b) accessibility, or (c) theoretical sampling? (Alternatively stated, was it a probabilistic, convenience, or theoretical sample?)
17. What information was given to subjects before, during, and after the study?
18. What were the subjects' social and emotional states before, during, and after the study?
19. What was the nature of the researcher's rapport with the subjects before, during, and after the study?

Data

20. What kinds of data and how much data were collected?
21. How were the data recorded?
22. What specific steps were followed in data collection?
23. What specific questions were asked?
24. Was there an interview agenda?
25. Were data transcribed, and if so, how?
26. Do the collected data fit with the researcher's general topic, theory, or applied issue?
27. Do the data adequately describe the study's focal concern or research issue?

Analysis

28. What techniques were applied, and were they adequately applied?
29. Did the analysis involve more global interpretations or more formalized analysis?

30. Is the analysis sufficiently described, such that it could be replicated based on the description?
31. If categories were developed, how were the categories defined?
32. If categories were defined, how were they imposed on the data?
33. Does the researcher's interpretation fit with what is already known about the research issue or applied problem?

Verification

34. What checks were implemented to allow the researcher to argue for *reliability*?
35. What controls were implemented to allow the researcher to discount bias and selective interpretations?
36. What arguments allow the researcher to imply *validity*?
37. What arguments allow the researcher to imply *generalizability*?

Discussion

38. Are the results clearly and concisely summarized and explained?
39. Do the study's implications follow closely or distantly from the data?
40. Are the study's limitations concisely stated?
41. Are the study's overall and specific contributions to the larger body of knowledge clearly and convincingly stated?
42. Are alternative explanations adequately considered?

References

Adler, P., & Adler, P. A. (1988). Intense loyalty in organizations: A case study of college athletics. *Administrative Science Quarterly, 33*, 401-417.

Agresti, A. (1990). *Categorical data analysis.* New York: John Wiley.

Agresti, A. (1996). *An introduction to categorical data analysis.* New York: John Wiley.

Aldrich, J. H., & Nelson, F. D. (1984). *Linear probability, logit, and probit models.* Beverly Hills, CA: Sage.

Barker, J. R. (1993). Tightening the iron cage: Concertive control in self-managing teams. *Administrative Science Quarterly, 38*, 61-103.

Barley, S. R. (1990). The alignment of technology and structure through roles and networks. *Administrative Science Quarterly, 35*, 61-103.

Bartunek, J. M. (1984). Changing interpretive schemes and organizational restructuring: The example of a religious order. *Administrative Science Quarterly, 29*, 355-372.

Biggart, N. W., & Hamilton, G. G. (1984). The power of obedience. *Administrative Science Quarterly, 29*, 540-549.

Bishop, Y. M. M., Fienberg, S. E., & Holland, P. W. (1975). *Discrete multivariate analysis.* Cambridge: MIT Press.

Blalock, H. M., Jr. (1982). *Conceptualization and measurement in the social sciences.* Beverly Hills, CA: Sage.

Briggs, P. (1988). What we know and what we need to know: The user model versus the user's model in human-computer interaction. *Behaviour and Information Technology, 7*, 431-442.

Briggs, P. (1990). Do they know what they're doing? An evaluation of word processing users' implicit and explicit task relevant knowledge and its role in self learning. *International Journal of Man-Machine Systems, 32*, 385-398.

177

Brown, S. L., & Eisenhardt, K. M. (1997). The art of continuous change: Linking complexity theory and time-paced evolution in relentlessly shifting organizations. *Administrative Science Quarterly, 43,* 1-34.

Burgelman, R. A. (1994). Fading memories: A process theory of strategic business exit in dynamic environments. *Administrative Science Quarterly, 39,* 24- 56.

Burgess, R. (1984). *In the field: An introduction to field research.* London: George Allen & Unwin.

Butterfield, K. D., Trevino, L. K., & Ball, G. A. (1996). Punishment from the manager's perspective: A grounded theory investigation and inductive model. *Academy of Management Journal, 39,* 1479-1512.

Campion, M. A. (1993). Article review checklist: A criterion checklist for reviewing research articles in applied psychology. *Personnel Psychology, 46,* 705-718.

Cassell, C., & Symon, G. (1994). Qualitative research in work contexts. In C. Cassell & G. Symon (Eds.), *Qualitative methods in organizational research: A practical guide* (pp. 1-13). London: Sage.

Coffey, A., & Atkinson, P. (1996). *Making sense of qualitative data: Complementary research strategies.* Thousand Oaks, CA: Sage.

Cohen, J., & Cohen, P. (1983). *Applied multiple regression/correlational analysis for the behavioral sciences* (2nd ed.). Hillsdale, NJ: Lawrence Erlbaum.

Connelly, F. M., & Clandinin, D. J. (1990). Stories of experience and narrative inquiry. *Educational Researcher, 19,* 2-14.

Cook, T. D., & Campbell, D. T. (1979). *Quasi-experimental design.* Palo Alto, CA: Houghton Mifflin.

Cox, D. R. (1970). *Analysis of binary data.* London: Chapman & Hall.

Creswell, J. W. (1994). *Research design.* Thousand Oaks, CA: Sage.

Creswell, J. W. (1998). *Qualitative inquiry and research design.* Thousand Oaks, CA: Sage.

DeMaris, A. (1992). *Logit modeling.* Newbury Park, CA: Sage.

Dollard, J. (1935). *Criteria for the life history.* New Haven, CT: Yale University Press.

Dutton, J. E., & Dukerich, J. M. (1991). Keeping an eye in the mirror: Image and identity in organizational adaptation. *Academy of Management Journal, 34,* 517-554.

Eisenhardt, K. M. (1989). Making fast decisions in high-velocity environments. *Academy of Management Journal, 32,* 543-576.

Elsbach, K. D., & Sutton, R. I. (1992). Acquiring organizational legitimacy through illegitimate actions: A marriage of institutional and impression management theories. *Academy of Management Journal, 35,* 699-738.

Ericsson, K. A., & Simon, H. A. (1984). *Protocol analysis: Verbal reports as data.* Cambridge: MIT Press.

Fienberg, S. E. (1989). *The analysis of cross-classified categorical data.* Cambridge: MIT Press.

Fondas, N. (1997). Feminization unveiled: Management qualities in contemporary writings. *Academy of Management Review, 22,* 257-282.

Forster, N. (1994). The analysis of company documentation. In C. Cassell & G. Symon (Eds.), *Qualitative methods in organizational research: A practical guide* (pp. 147-166). London: Sage.

Gammack, J. G., & Stephens, R. A. (1994). Repertory grid technique in constructive interaction. In C. Cassell & G. Symon (Eds.), *Qualitative methods in organizational research: A practical guide* (pp. 72-90). London: Sage.

Gatewood, R. D., & Feild, H. S. (1994). *Human resources selection* (3rd ed.). New York: Dryden.

Gersick, C. J. G. (1988). Time and transition in work teams: Toward a new model of group development. *Academy of Management Journal, 31,* 9-41.

Ghiselli, E. E. (1964). *Theory of psychological measurement.* New York: McGraw-Hill.

Ghiselli, E. E., Campbell, J. P., & Zedeck, S. (1981). *Measurement theory for the behavioral sciences.* San Francisco: Freeman.

Glaser, B. G. (1992). *Basics of grounded theory analysis.* Mill Valley, CA: Sociological Press.

Glaser, B. G., & Strauss, A. L. (1967). *The discovery of grounded theory: Strategies for qualitative research.* Chicago: Aldine.

Glaserfeld, E. V. (1984). An introduction to radical constructivism. In P. Watzlawick (Ed.), *The invented reality.* New York: Norton.

Gorsuch, R. L. (1974). *Factor analysis.* Philadelphia: Saunders.

Greenwood, R., Hinings, C. R., & Brown, J. (1994). Merging professional service firms. *Organizational Science, 5,* 239-257.

Guilford, J. P., & Fruchter, B. (1973). *Fundamental statistics in psychology and education* (5th ed.). New York: McGraw-Hill.

Hackman, J. R., & Oldham, G. R. (1980). *Work redesign.* Reading, MA: Addison-Wesley.

Hamel, G. (1991). Competition for competence and interpartner learning within international strategic alliances. *Strategic Management Journal, 12,* 83- 103.

Harvey, R. J. (1991). Job analysis. In M. D. Dunnette & L. M. Hough (Eds.), *Handbook of industrial and organizational psychology* (Vol. 2, 2nd ed., pp. 71-163). Palo Alto, CA: Consulting Psychologists Press.

Hom, P. W., & Griffeth, R. W. (1995). *Employee turnover.* Cincinnati, OH: Southwestern.

Hornby, P., & Symon, G. (1994). Tracer studies. In C. Cassell & G. Symon (Eds.), *Qualitative methods in organizational research: A practical guide* (pp. 167-186). London: Sage.

Hosmer, D. W., & Lemeshow, S. (1989). *Applied logistic regression.* New York: John Wiley.

Hout, M. (1983). *Mobility tables.* Beverly Hills, CA: Sage.

Human, S. E., & Provan, K. (1997). An emergent theory of structure and outcomes in small-firm strategic manufacturing networks. *Academy of Management Journal, 40,* 368-402.

Hundley, G., Jacobson, C. K., & Park, S. H. (1996). Effects of profitability and liquidity on R&D intensity: Japanese and U.S. companies compared. *Academy of Management Journal, 39,* 1659-1674.

Ilgen, D. R., & Hollenbeck, J. R. (1991). The structure of work: Job design and roles. In M. D. Dunnette & L. M. Hough (Eds.), *Handbook of industrial and organizational psychology* (Vol. 2, 2nd ed., pp. 165-207). Palo Alto, CA: Consulting Psychologists Press.

Johnson, G. I., & Briggs, P. (1994). Question-asking and verbal protocol techniques. In C. Cassell & G. Symon (Eds.), *Qualitative methods in organizational research: A practical guide* (pp. 55-71). London: Sage.

Kelly, G. A. (1955). *The psychology of personal constructs.* New York: Norton.

Kuhn, T. S. (1996). *The structure of scientific revolutions* (3rd ed.). Chicago: University of Chicago Press.

Kvale, S. (1996). *InterViews: An introduction to qualitative research interviewing.* Thousand Oaks, CA: Sage.

Larsson, R., & Lowendahl, B. (1996, August). *The qualitative side of management research.* Paper presented at the annual meeting of the Academy of Management, Cincinnati, OH.

Lee, T. W., & Mitchell, T. R. (1994). An alternative approach: The unfolding model of voluntary employee turnover. *Academy of Management Review, 19,* 51-89.

Lee, T. W., Mitchell, T. R., Wise, L., & Fireman, S. (1996). An unfolding model of voluntary employee turnover. *Academy of Management Journal, 39,* 5-36.

Lincoln, Y. S., & Guba, E. G. (1985). *Naturalistic inquiry.* Beverly Hills, CA: Sage.

Locke, K. (1996). Rewriting *The discovery of grounded theory* after 25 years. *Journal of Management Inquiry, 5,* 239-245.

Loscocco, K. A. (1997). Work-family linkages among self-employed women and men. *Journal of Vocational Behavior, 50,* 204-226.

Mangione, T. W. (1995). *Mail surveys.* Thousand Oaks, CA: Sage.

Marshall, C., & Rossman, G. B. (1995). *Designing qualitative research* (2nd ed.). Thousand Oaks, CA: Sage.

Mason, J. (1996). *Qualitative researching.* Thousand Oaks, CA: Sage.

Maurer, S. D., Howe, V., & Lee, T. W. (1992). Organizational recruiting as marketing management: An interdisciplinary study of engineering graduates. *Personnel Psychology, 45,* 807-834.

Maxwell, J. A. (1996). *Qualitative research design.* Thousand Oaks, CA: Sage.

McCall, M. W., & Bobko, P. (1990). Research methods in the service of discovery. In M. D. Dunnette & L. M. Hough (Eds.), *Handbook of industrial and organizational psychology* (Vol. 1, pp. 381-418). Palo Alto, CA: Consulting Psychologists Press.

Mead, G. H. (1934). *Mind, self, and society: From the standpoint of a social behaviorist.* Chicago: University of Chicago Press.

Menard, S. (1995). *Applied logistic regression.* Thousand Oaks, CA: Sage.

Merton, R. K., Fiske, M., & Kendall, P. L. (1990). *The focused interview* (2nd ed.). New York: Free Press.

Miles, M. B., & Huberman, A. M. (1994). *Qualitative data analysis: An expanded sourcebook* (2nd ed.). Thousand Oaks, CA: Sage.

Mintzberg, H. (1994). *The rise and fall of strategic planning.* New York: Free Press.

Morgan, D. L. (1995). Why things (sometimes) go wrong in focus groups. *Qualitative Health Research, 5,* 515-522.

Morgan, D. L. (1997). *Focus groups as qualitative research.* Thousand Oaks, CA: Sage.

Morita, J. G., Lee, T. W., & Mowday, R. T. (1989). Introducing survival analysis to organizational researchers: A selected application to turnover research. *Journal of Applied Psychology, 74,* 280-292.

Morita, J. G., Lee, T. W., & Mowday, R. T. (1993). The regression-analog to survival analysis: A selected application to turnover research. *Academy of Management Journal, 36,* 1430-1464.

Mossman, D., Holly, F., & Schnoor, J. (1991). Field observations of longitudinal dispersion in a run-of-the-water river impoundment. *Water Research, 25,* 1405-1415.

Mowday, R. T. (1992). Out of the tangled thicket: Persistence in the face of failed conventional wisdom. In P. Frost & R. Stablein (Eds.), *Doing exemplary research* (pp. 129-135). Newbury Park, CA: Sage.

Mowday, R. T., Steers, R. M., & Porter, L. W. (1979). The measurement of organizational commitment. *Journal of Vocational Behavior, 14,* 224-247.

Noer, D. M. (1993). *Healing the wounds.* San Francisco: Jossey-Bass.

Nunnally, J. C. (1978). *Psychometric theory* (2nd ed.). New York: McGraw-Hill.

Pierce, J. L., Gardner, D. G., Cummings, L. L., & Dunham, R. B. (1989). Organization-based self-esteem: Construct definition, measurement, and validation. *Academy of Management Journal, 32,* 622-648.

Pratt, M. G., & Rafaeli, A. (1997). Organizational dress as a symbol of multilayered social identities. *Academy of Management Journal, 40,* 862-898.

Rees, A., & Nicholson, N. (1994). The twenty statements test. In C. Cassell & G. Symon (Eds.), *Qualitative methods in organizational research: A practical guide* (pp. 37-54). London: Sage.

Rhodes, S. R., & Steers, R. M. (1990). *Managing employee absenteeism.* Menlo Park, CA: Addison-Wesley.

Roberts, K. H., Hulin, C. L., & Rousseau, D. M. (1978). *Developing an interdisciplinary science of organizations.* San Francisco: Jossey-Bass.

Ross, J., & Staw, B. M. (1986). Expo 86: An escalation prototype. *Administrative Science Quarterly, 31,* 274-297.

Rynes, S. L., Bretz, R. D., & Gerhart, B. (1991). The importance of recruitment in job choice: A different way of looking. *Personnel Psychology, 44,* 487-521.

Schwab, D. P. (1980). Construct validity in organizational behavior. In B. M. Staw & L. L. Cummings (Eds.), *Research in organizational behavior* (Vol. 2, pp. 3-43). Greenwich, CT: JAI.

Spitzer, S., Couch, C., & Stratton, J. (1973). *The assessment of self.* Iowa City: Sernoll.

Staw, B. M. (1992). Do smiles lead to sales? Comments on the Sutton/Rafaeli study. In P. Frost & R. Stablein (Eds.), *Doing exemplary research* (pp. 136-140). Newbury Park, CA: Sage.

Staw, B. M., Barsade, S. G., & Koput, K. W. (1997). Escalation at the credit window: A longitudinal study of bank executives' recognition and write-off of problem loans. *Journal of Applied Psychology, 82,* 130-142.

Strauss, A. L. (1987). *Qualitative analysis for social scientists.* New York: Cambridge University Press.

Sutton, R. I. (1991). Maintaining organizational norms about expressed emotions: The case of bill collectors. *Administrative Science Quarterly, 36,* 245-268.

Sutton, R. I., & Hargadon, A. (1996). Brainstorming groups in context: Effectiveness in a product design firm. *Administrative Science Quarterly, 41,* 685-718.

Sutton, R. I., & Rafaeli, A. (1988). Untangling the relationship between displayed emotions and organizational sales: The case of convenience stores. *Academy of Management Journal, 31,* 461-487.

Sutton, R. I., & Rafaeli, A. (1992). How we untangled the relationship between displayed emotion and organizational sales: A tale of bickering and optimism. In P. Frost & R. Stablein (Eds.), *Doing exemplary research* (pp. 115-128). Newbury Park, CA: Sage.

Thomas, J. (1993). *Doing critical ethnography.* Newbury Park, CA: Sage.

U.S. Department of Labor, Employment and Training Division. (1991). *Dictionary of occupational titles* (4th ed.). Washington, DC: Government Printing Office.

U.S. Department of Labor, Manpower Administration. (1972). *Handbook for analyzing jobs.* Washington, DC: Government Printing Office.

Van Dyne, L., Graham, J. W., & Dienesch, R. M. (1994). Organizational citizenship behavior: Construct redefinition, measurement, and validation. *Academy of Management Journal, 37,* 765-802.

Van Maanen, J. (1975). Police socialization. *Administrative Science Quarterly, 20,* 207-228.

Vaughan, D. (1990). Autonomy, interdependence, and social control: NASA and the space shuttle *Challenger. Administrative Science Quarterly, 35,* 225- 257.

Waddington, D. (1994). Participant observation. In C. Cassell & G. Symon (Eds.), *Qualitative methods in organizational research: A practical guide* (pp. 107-122). London: Sage.

Walsh, K. (1978). *Neuropsychology: A clinical approach.* Edinburgh: Churchill Livingstone.

Weick, K. E. (1995). *Sensemaking in organizations.* Thousand Oaks, CA: Sage.

Wheeler, M. A., Stuss, D. T., & Tulving, E. (1997). Toward a theory of episodic memory: The frontal lobes and autonoetic consciousness. *Psychological Bulletin, 121,* 371-394.

Yamaguchi, K. (1991). *Event history analysis.* Newbury Park, CA: Sage.

Yan, A., & Gray, B. (1994). Bargaining power, management control, and performance in United States-China joint ventures: A comparative case study. *Academy of Management Journal, 37,* 1478-1517.

Yin, R. K. (1984). *Case study research: Design and methods.* Beverly Hills, CA: Sage.

Yin, R. K. (1994). *Case study research: Design and methods* (2nd ed.). Thousand Oaks, CA: Sage.

Zabusky, S. E., & Barley, S. R. (1997). "You can't be a stone if you're cement": Reevaluating the emic identities of scientists in organizations. In L. L. Cummings & B. M. Staw (Eds.), *Research in organizational behavior* (Vol. 19, pp. 361-404). Greenwich, CT: JAI.

Index

Academy of Management meetings, 2, 3
Adler, P., 15, 21, 23, 27, 100
Adler, P. A., 15, 21, 23, 27, 100
Agresti, A., 8, 13, 123, 126, 127, 137, 141
Aldrich, J. H., 137
Analytic generalization, 156, 158-159
Archival methods, 22, 23, 24, 172
   content analysis, 24
   histories, 24
   literary criticism, 24
Atkinson, P., 28, 29, 31, 32, 35, 97, 100
Audiovisual data presentation, 95, 96, 98,
     113-115
   films, 114
   strengths, 114
   weaknesses, 114

Ball, G. A., 9, 24
Barker, J. R., 15
Barley, S. R., 15, 16, 40
Barsade, S. G., 152
Bartunek, J. M., 15
Biggart, N. W., 15
Biserial correlation, 129, 131-132, 134, 135
   standard error, 132

Bishop, Y.M.M., 8
Blalock, H. M., Jr., 145
Bobko, P., 10
Bretz, R. D., 40
Briggs, P., 101, 103, 104, 105
Brown, J., 15
Brown, S. L., 21
Burgelman, R. A., 15
Burgess, R., 98
Butterfield, K. D., 9, 24

Campbell, D. T., 78
Campbell, J. P., 147
Campion, M. A., 174
Case studies, 22, 38, 41
Case study research, 15, 54-61, 94, 172
   main components, 58-60
   main purpose, 54
   research questions, 58-59
   "shock to the system," 55
   strength, 78-79
   tested theory, 55-56
   test of unfolding model, 57-58
   theoretical propositions, 59
   theory generation, 60

About the Author

Thomas W. Lee is Professor of Human Resource Management and Organizational Behavior in the Department of Management and Organization, School of Business Administration, University of Washington, Seattle. He earned his Ph.D. at the University of Oregon, his M.A. at Bowling Green State University, and his A.B. at the University of California, Berkeley. He currently serves on the editorial boards of *Human Resource Management Review, Journal of Management, Organizational Research Methods, and Personnel Psychology,* and he formerly served on the editorial boards of the *Academy of Management Journal* and *Journal of Management Inquiry.* His work has appeared in the *Academy of Management Journal, Academy of Management Review, Human Resource Management Review, Industrial Relations, Journal of Applied Psychology, Journal of Management, Journal of Vocational Behavior, Motivation and Emotion,* and *Personnel Psychology.* Prior to pursuing an academic career, he worked for the Southern California Edison Company in Rosemead, California. He is married and has one son. His e-mail address is orcas@u.washington.edu.

AEG 9160

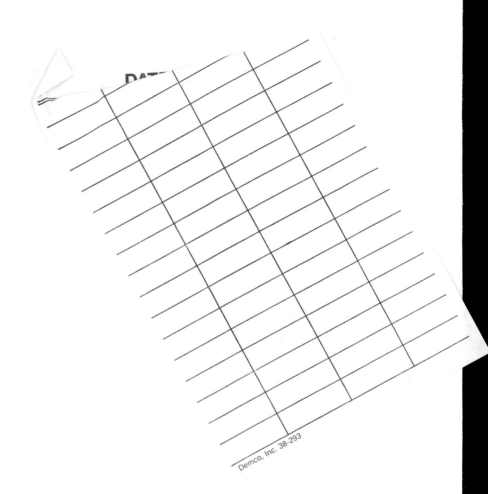